THE POWER OF FAITH

This book is a compilation of messages given by David Hathaway in his meetings and conferences between 1994 and 2004, forged out of his experience with God over a lifetime. He wants this book to inspire and motivate you to get a vision of the God of the impossible, who can do the impossible.

The Power of Faith

DAVID HATHAWAY

Eurovision

THANKFUL BOOKS

First published 2004

Published by Thankful Books
70 Milton Road, Eastbourne, East Sussex BN21 1SS

ISBN: 1 905084 01 3

Scripture references that are not
paraphrased are taken from the King
James Version.

Note: *Eurovision*, referred to in the text and introduced
in the end pages of this book, is the short name of *Eurovision
Mission to Europe*, Registered Charity No. 1013288.

Book design and production for the publisher by
Bookprint Creative Services, P.O. Box 827, BN21 3YJ, England.
Printed in Great Britain.

CONTENTS

FOREWORD

This is quite some book, and quite some author! Who else is ministering from this country and seeing thousands of miraculous healings and conversions through Jesus Christ? Is it just in Russia, or can it happen here too?

America honours men like Billy Graham, but here we 'keep 'em obscure and poor'. Nevertheless, *by their fruits shall ye know them*, and I have realised that we can no longer ignore David Hathaway and this *Eurovision* ministry.

I wonder what part Russia will take in the end of history, and how it will affect Israel. Don't write off Russia. It is the biggest land-mass nation in the world, twice as big as the second largest – Canada. Russia's minerals include gold, and it is the European country with the oil and gas for the future.

David Hathaway is not just leaving behind thousands of converts and healed people in Russia. *Eurovision*'s team is responsible for much of the church leadership of Russia, for the future. That could change the course of history.

And what of this book? It challenges you and me to change our lives. There must be a way that we can release our God of the whole universe, to save and heal our loved ones, our families, our friends and the people we know.

I think this book will help ordinary Christians like you and me – businessmen and businesswomen, mums, dads, brothers, sisters and so on.

The Power of Faith makes uncomfortable reading and that's a good thing. I still love Jesus Christ and I want to serve Him until my time on earth is done. What about you? As for me, I want to learn from this man, this ministry and this book – because it all comes back to Jesus.

Gareth Littler
Director, Centre for Justice and Liberty
July 2004

INTRODUCTION

A VISION AND A MINISTRY FOR OVER 50 YEARS

Son of a pioneer of the early Pentecostal movement in Great Britain, David Hathaway's life is characterised from the very beginning by a desperate, impatient desire to experience personally and to demonstrate publicly who the REAL Jesus is. Everyone knows about religion, but they don't know who the REAL Jesus is.

David has always chosen to live on the edge, in the danger zone, to take amazing risks for God. Miraculously released from a communist prison, healed of cancer twice, almost killed on five occasions, and through many other miracles, he is still proving that life with Christ is an unfolding adventure. He says he would rather live in a storm with Jesus than live at peace without Him.

Asked to pastor a church at 18, just three months after starting Bible college, and holding his first tent mission a few months later, David Hathaway has seen the power of God and miracles of healing from the very beginning of his ministry.

After ten years as a full-time pastor and evangelist in

Britain, David's ministry to Russia and Europe began in 1961 when he organised the first post-war overland expedition to Jerusalem, travelling behind the Iron Curtain through the Arab countries and into Israel. He had heard that there was to be a World Pentecostal Conference in Jerusalem on the Day of Pentecost! Full of expectation of what God would do, he determined to be there. He had no money to go, but was challenged to do the impossible – set up an expedition, go by road!

Everyone from the motoring organisations to the British Foreign Office said it was too dangerous: there were the hazards of crossing the Iron Curtain countries, on unknown roads, without suitable hotels – in Turkey they could be killed by bandits, and in Syria shot as spies – and it was impossible to make the two-way crossing by road in and out of Israel! Even David's own father (Rev W G Hathaway), a man of faith, prayed desperately that God would stop him! But David's heart was set because he believed that if he went by faith, revival would come and he himself would experience a new personal Pentecost.

David went. Revival did not come in the conference, but God lit a fire in David's soul, an unquenchable passion which grows stronger every year for God's power to be demonstrated in those lands he crossed.

The overland expedition to Israel generated so much interest among Christians that David was almost forced to set up his own travel company to Israel: Crusader Tours. With official licences to travel all over Eastern Europe, it was while crossing communist Europe that David saw the desperate spiritual need and God gave him a vision for Russia and the Soviet dominated countries. Burning in his heart was a desire for a revival greater than the world has ever seen – after all, the people of Central and Eastern Europe have never, since the day of Christ, seen the real power of God, but for 2000 years have been enslaved by either religion or ideology. This vision and call was confirmed in 1964 by a miraculous healing from throat cancer. David began smuggling Bibles in a secret compartment on his buses – he could take in two tonnes of Bibles every time! But on Midsummer's day 1972, after taking in over 150,000 Bibles and New Testaments, David was stopped at the Czechoslovak border with 5000 Bibles destined for Russia. He was arrested, tortured and sentenced to five years in prison – then another five years for preaching the Gospel inside the prison!

In answer to prayer, God showed him the exact day of his release and, after ten months in prison, by a miracle God sent the British Prime Minister, Harold Wilson, to bring him out! This miracle and his experience with God in the prison meant that before returning to work in Eastern Europe, David told his story around the world, leading more than a quarter of a million people to Christ in just two years.

After his release from prison, David's heart continued to burn for Eastern Europe, the last words of one of his fellow prisoners continually ringing in his ears: 'David, don't forget us. No one knows, no one in the West cares.' In 1976 he organised the successful worldwide campaign for the release of Georgi Vins, a renowned Russian pastor from Kiev, sentenced to long years in a Siberian prison for his faith. David continued to go into the underground churches to preach until eventually, in the 1980s, he began to openly hold crusades and conferences in the communist countries.

But it was in 1986 that God spoke clearly to David again, telling him that the Iron Curtain that had separated East and West Europe for so long would be melted by the power of the Holy Spirit; that a new great move of the Spirit would sweep across the whole of Europe, uniting East and West; that this would not be an act of man, but a sovereign act of God, moving in such demonstration that it could only be recognised as the Holy Spirit's power.

God challenged David to hold an 'East-West' conference in Karlsruhe, West Germany. In 1988 he began to see the vision and prophecy fulfilled when 4000 delegates came to the first conference – and 600 came by a miracle through the Iron Curtain! God challenged David to hold a second East-West conference in 1989, publicly prophesying the fall of the Curtain. Six hundred came from the East, and within a few days of the ending of the conference, the Iron Curtain began to fall!

David's ministry, then known as *Crusader International Mission to Europe*, organised and hosted these East-West *Eurovision* conferences. In the first conference in 1988, Pastors John and Dodie Osteen from Lakewood Church, Texas, USA, along with Reinhard Bonnke, were the main speakers. One day, Dodie Osteen pointed to the big *Eurovision* banner outside the hall and said, 'David, *Eurovision* is YOUR vision!'

David did not understand then what God was saying to him, but it was true – God had given him a new, powerful and life-changing vision for Europe that had begun to unfold in front of him like a scroll: first the revelation of the opening of the Iron Curtain, then following the thousands of East Europeans back across the borders, evangelising in the stadiums in Hungary, Bulgaria and Romania, followed by the first crusades and conferences in Ukraine, followed by the great crusades in Siberia, and now all over Russia.

In the first ten years after the East-West conferences, David personally held over 300 evangelistic missions in the former Soviet countries with hundreds of thousands of people saved. In just one five-year period, over 20,000 miracles of healing were recorded.

In 1995, David launched *Prophetic Vision* magazine. Nine years later, the readership is over half a million – one of the largest Christian readerships in the world! The aim of the magazine is to convey the strong prophetic vision David has concerning Europe, the Middle East and Russia, so clear that it is like looking down on a map of the devil's strategy, but also God's strategy – what He wants to do. David's intention is to challenge the church to act NOW, to make evangelism the priority – NOW!

As a direct result of an armed attack on David in Ukraine on 2 June 1998, intended to stop him ever evangelising there again, *Eurovision International TV Company* was formed. By a miracle, in answer to strong prophetic intercessory prayer the day before, David was not shot as had been planned. To maximise publicity after the attack, and hopefully see the return of his stolen vehicle and its contents, David called a press conference. Amazed by the positive response both in the press and on TV, God gave David the vision that if the authorities wanted to stop him evangelising in auditoriums and stadiums, he could reach the whole nation through the media, as every home has a TV set as part of the old Soviet propaganda system.

So by faith David went into production at once, borrowing staff and equipment from the local TV station in Lvov, the very town where he had been attacked. The first evangelistic programme, *The Power of Faith*, was ready by the end of that same month, before he had even left the country!

Having begun by faith, God worked another miracle for David, and blessed him with a gift of the latest television equipment to fulfil the vision of preparing and broadcasting top quality professional TV Gospel programmes! Ordered from Italy, the equipment crossed the Ukraine border just after New Year 1999, but characteristically a new law had just been passed which made all the carefully prepared import documents invalid, leaving the truck with its invaluable cargo stranded in the snow at the border. We needed another miracle urgently! After much prayer, three weeks later the equipment was under customs seal in Kiev, but it was only on 26 May 1999 that all the complicated documentation was finally completed and the TV equipment could be unloaded into our new studio – legally imported with only nominal customs duty.

In the first twelve months of operating out of a tiny studio (only 57 square metres), *Eurovision International TV Company* produced 38 evangelistic programmes, covering 75 per cent of the Ukraine with David's weekly broadcast on regional terrestrial TV channels. Programming continues non-stop.

The programme series called *The Power of Faith* is well received by the viewers, by the local authorities (who take a great interest in religious matters) and by the local TV companies in Russia and Ukraine. In Ukraine the programme now goes out to the whole nation on Saturdays on national TV. David is able to show what God is doing among their people; how God is manifesting His power in their country, and healing their sick by miracles. This is not

'Christian' TV programming, but real crusade evangelism, a real demonstration of the power of God touching real people, and because of David's many years of ministry in Russia and Ukraine and his real love for the people, the viewers respond to this. At the end of each programme a six-part Bible correspondence course for new believers is offered free to all those accepting Christ. *The Power of Faith* 30-minute Gospel programmes are also shown every week via several non-subscription satellite channels (TBN Europe, Life-TV and CNL) reaching all Europe, including the Baltic States, parts of Africa and the Middle East.

In 2002, God gave David a new powerful vision to evangelise Russia. Realising that still less than half of 1 per cent of the Russian population are baptised believers, he was discouraged. This was the challenge God gave: to go into the cities with the largest churches in Russia, to evangelise in a sports hall/stadium and to buy air time on TV, to broadcast the WHOLE evangelistic meeting live, reaching the ENTIRE region (between 1 and 5 million every time) via terrestrial TV – direct into every town, every village, every home, every apartment – using the TV system set up by the communists for propaganda! In the first 14 months of launching this programme, David held 20 live TV crusades, double the number he had originally planned!

The live crusade programmes show the praise and worship, the unedited preaching, the call to repentance and, in the last twelve minutes, healing miracles! Outside the big cities, in the regions, there are usually only one or two TV channels, so the programme has a great impact: the majority of people within the whole region, if they switch on their TV, will see the programme. Many get healed and give their lives to Christ. Some of these then come into the actual crusade meeting in the following days to give their testimony! In the Mukachevo region of West Ukraine, the television company estimated that 90 per cent of the one and a half million population watched the crusade broadcast in March 2003. So many people called the TV station afterwards, wanting to see the programmes all over again, that the TV director re-broadcast the crusade five times, FREE!

Following the launch of the live TV broadcasts, David was diagnosed with lung cancer. He was faced with a challenge: did he really believe God or not? The doctors fast tracked him into a process which would lead to an operation to remove part if not all of his right lung. David prayed, 'Lord, how can I go back into Russia and preach like I preach and say that You are the God of the impossible, a mighty God of miracles who's got power to do everything, including heal cancer, if I have half of my right lung cut out? If You have finished with me, if my ministry is over, then don't heal me, because if I can no longer evangelise, I might as well die. I have no other reason to live! But if You want me to go back into Russia and Ukraine and finish the work You gave me to do, then I want You to heal me completely!'

David only had a few days left, from Thursday to Monday, then the doctors were going to operate. God said, 'David, you've got a mountain in your life that you've got to move, and that mountain is to get that cancer out from your lung. If you can believe that without an operation you can be completely healed, then nothing will be impossible for you from there on.'

On the Monday David was in the hospital, tubes down

his lung as the doctors looked for the cancer, but God had already given him the answer. He knew it was gone! The doctors looked at David in amazement – they were shocked – and said, 'You have no cancer!'

In 2004, God gave a new and greater vision: to hold the largest crusade ever in Russia, or indeed in Europe – ten consecutive days of evangelism broadcast live on TV from five cities, linking seven regions, over-filled stadiums, hundreds of thousands converted, thousands of miracles! Not by cable or by satellite, but by using the terrestrial TV the communists provided, so that all could hear the Gospel of Jesus Christ and see the glory of God as the miracles happened before their own eyes!

The vision continues to grow. David says, 'I will not stop until we reach the whole of Russia with the Gospel of Jesus Christ. It takes revolutionary faith that will overcome every challenge. But with God and your support we can do it!'

After a lifetime of evangelising, David still issues the same challenge to all believers: 'Every Christian should be on their knees crying out to God; everyone should be evangelising. You should be out there preaching the Gospel. I am a revolutionary – sometimes I think we should close the churches and send everybody out onto the streets to preach the Gospel! You see, when the fire and power of God comes down, it will shake men and women, get them out of their seats to do something. That is what God is doing to me. God is shaking me, God is driving me by the Holy Ghost. There is a church in Ukraine who were turned out of their rented theatre because of one of my crusades. The city authorities were so angry, that the church was forced to meet in the street in the middle of winter with temperatures of minus 25 degrees! The church was on the street, but they did not stop evangelising – they preached the Gospel to more people! As a result the church grew rapidly. Now the city became really angry. They said, "We can't allow you to preach in the street. This is far too dangerous," and forced the church back into the theatre! Can you imagine that happening to you? The authorities close your church, you preach in the street, thousands more people come, and then they make you go back into your building! That is the way to fill your church. Try it! But it takes faith!'

Eurovision Mission to Europe
July 2004

Part I

Faith in Action!

CHAPTER ONE

I BELIEVE IN ACTION

I want to challenge you to rise up and do something for the glory of God in the power of the Holy Ghost and in the Name of Jesus. We're living in a time of real spiritual warfare; of not just saying, 'Oh, I'm going to bind the power of the devil,' but getting out there where the devil is and trouncing him head-on until we get the victory!

I believe in action. God has called us into the kingdom, and if you are a born-again, baptised, Spirit-filled believer, God has done that for a reason. God doesn't save you and call you so that you can sit at ease. We are saved to serve! Not just to have a wonderful life.

We don't all have to be preachers, but the fact is that we are saved to live for God. He has called us, but we have to make it happen! I believe in prayer, and I believe in miracles, but miracles happen when God uses men and women to work the miracles. I hear people all over the world say, 'Oh, it's not the time for evangelism, and if God wants to save people, He will do it Himself.' No, God sent His Son into the world to die on the cross to set the world free, but we've got to declare it! It's no use just sitting there. God needs people. He needs people to give financially – especially He needs businessmen who will turn their businesses over to work for Him and produce money for the Kingdom. God will honour and prosper businessmen when they get that vision to devote their money to winning souls. And we need people who will intercede and pray – I couldn't achieve what I do without people all over the world who are interceding and praying. And we need the preachers.

Moses in Exodus 3 was a very ordinary man, busy doing a job, keeping the flock of Jethro, his father-in-law. And as he led the flock to the back of the desert, to Horeb, the angel of the Lord appeared to him in a flame of fire out of the midst of a bush. Moses looked, and the bush burned but was not consumed. Sometimes God has to do something unusual in our lives to attract our attention, to make us turn aside from the cares of the world, from the responsibilities that we have, from those business problems, from our sickness, our pain and all those other problems we've got. God wants us to turn aside like Moses and look at Him.

I want you to understand: if God is going to deal with you, if God is going to call you, if God is going to use you – and God wants to use every one of you – if you're not in a position where He can use you, then examine your spiritual life and ask the question: Why am I saved? Because you are saved to serve!

One of the most moving things about the Queen's 50-year Jubilee celebration was the fact that she is the wealthiest woman in Britain, with more power and prestige than anyone, yet she acknowledged her call before God to serve the nation. Jesus said, 'Let him who would be the greatest among you, be your servant,' and for those of us looking for honour and esteem, and those of us looking for position in spiritual life, let me remind you that 'position' begins with servanthood – 'let them become your servant'.

I want to emphasise that God called me. I did not choose to serve God. Jesus said in His own words, 'You did not choose me. I chose you.' He called us in order that we might serve Him, and I believe that He called every single born-again believer to serve Him. And once you are called into service you will need the Holy Spirit's fire and power, because you cannot make it on your own.

I remember the day when the Lord challenged me to serve Him. I was 15, on holiday on the South Coast of England, walking on the seafront with some young Christians, and I couldn't enter into the fun that they were having because God was speaking to me – and the devil was speaking to me. The devil was saying, 'Don't listen. It's OK, things are fine. You're doing well. You got saved when you were 8, and you got baptised in water when you were 12. You started preaching at 13. That's enough,' and God was saying, 'I want more.' God was not calling me to be a preacher or an evangelist at that time. God was asking me to give my whole life to Him. Simply to give everything to Him.

I remember the battle that summer's evening, as the sun began to go down. It became such a strong battle that I had to separate myself from the others. The devil was saying, 'Don't do it. You're doing enough – don't do any more,' and God was saying, 'I want you, David. I want everything you have and everything you are.' At that moment God did not say, 'You're going to be a preacher; you're going to be an evangelist; you're going to be a missionary.' It was to say, 'David, I want all – or nothing.' And I was just 15 years old!

That's where we begin with God – it's all or nothing. You can't play with God, you can't fool with Him. What are you called for? Are you called to live for God, or for yourself? To have a good time, a family and a big house, a car and a successful business and just to go on until your pension comes? No, when God called you, He said, 'I want everything, including your success.'

I understood that night on the beach that God was trying to get my attention. One of the battles God has is to get our attention, and with Moses God had to do something extraordinary. Moses was looking after the sheep – he had got himself married, had some kids and was busy, tied up with all the problems that you have, working hard to get enough money to feed his growing family – when suddenly, out in the desert, God appeared to him in a burning bush. What attracted Moses was not that the bush was on fire but that the fire didn't burn it. There is a time when the fire of God will burn up the impurities in your life, but when He starts to put the fire into you, He does not want to destroy you, He wants to use the real you! God knows who you are. Sometimes when I am having problems, and I have to say – like Paul – 'Lord, I am sorry. I should have done this and I shouldn't have done that,' and when I am trying to make excuses and say, 'I'm not perfect, I can't do this, and Lord, You know the problems I have in my life,' God says, 'Look, I knew you before you were born. I made you and it's about time you understood I made you, just as you are, for a purpose.'

God was calling Moses: 'I want you to go to Pharaoh and tell him, "Let My people go." Just do it.' Please understand – Moses was a human being, no different from you. All right, he was born into a humble family but adopted by a woman of wealth, and then he had some problems and now is living in relative poverty out in the desert, with a family and responsibilities like you, so he's human! And he argued with God, 'Look, when I talk to my own people, let alone Pharaoh, they won't listen to me!' (Exodus 4:1).

How did God convince Moses? God's answer was very simple: 'What is it you have got in your hand?' God took the ordinary common thing Moses had in his hand, his shepherd's rod, and used that as the demonstration. God will use those troubles, those tribulations, those difficulties, those everyday things that you have in your life, to speak to you. When I think of the number of troubles I have had – being in a communist prison for a year, having cancer twice, having gunmen sent on three occasions to shoot me – God uses every circumstance to His glory; He uses the problems and the difficulties in our lives to convince us miraculously!

With Moses, first God had to use the miracle of the burning bush to attract his attention, and secondly, in Exodus 4:3, He commanded Moses, 'Throw your rod on the ground.' He did and it became a serpent. Moses fled – he was afraid! The problem is so many people are afraid when they see the power of God and run away from the reality of what God wants to do in their lives. You have got to WANT the miracle! Why do I see miracles? I WANT miracles, I LIVE for miracles. I live to see the glory and the power of God! Often it's difficult, but I won't give up. I won't let go of God until He works the miracles, because God cannot fail.

In the West you can live even as a Christian without one

iota of faith. From the cradle to the grave, you can get medical and financial benefit from the state like anyone else. OK, it's not much, but if you are in difficulty you can find help without faith. That is why if you want real faith, God may have to bring some major crisis into your life to get your attention. I thank God for the crises in my life because that's how I have learnt faith, and how I have learnt to trust God, and that's why miracles happen.

But first we must start with a servant's heart. We are saved to serve Him!

CHAPTER TWO

THE COMMAND AND THE FIRE OF GOD

I want to share with you something that God has been saying strongly to ME since 1992 and which is powerfully motivating MY life. And I want to give YOU the same strong spiritual challenge which Moses gave to Israel in Deuteronomy 4:32 – 'Ask now of the days that are past, since the day that God created man on the earth, and ask from the one side of Heaven to the other, WHETHER THERE HAS BEEN ANY SUCH THING AS THIS GREAT THING IS, OR HAS BEEN HEARD LIKE IT?' I have not found any other man who could make a statement as strong as this; that Israel had witnessed the greatest miracle ever! Yes, this was 3000 years ago, but I believe that it also relates to today, and will be EXCEEDED in Russia – which is why I evangelise there!

At the time of speaking, Moses is 120 years old, but 40 years before this something had happened which brought a bigger change to the nation of Israel than anything ever experienced in any nation before or since: the moment when God, for the first time, began to demonstrate the greatness of His power by working the most outstanding, visible miracles in front of the most powerful nation in the whole earth.

Moses asks the people a question in two dimensions – time and space. First Moses says, from the very beginning of time until now, has anyone ever witnessed a miracle as big as this – the biggest, most earth-shaking demonstration of God's power ever seen? Secondly Moses says, ask the question in space, from one side of the world to the other, from America to Russia, from the north to the south – in the whole world – has ever any man seen a greater miracle than this happen, visibly, on earth? The answer is no! It is the greatest miracle ever. And it happened just 40 years ago. What was it?

This is the background: God chose a baby, born to a slave woman, who became the son of the king's daughter by the plan of God. Later, he saw an Egyptian beating one of his fellow Israelites and killed him. As a result he fled Egypt to escape justice. He married, had a family, looked after sheep and worked for his father-in-law until he was 80 years old. Now suddenly God called this man, saying, 'Go back to the place that you came from, challenge the greatest leader in the world, the most powerful nation on earth, demand that they release your persecuted, suffering people. Command Pharaoh to let them go!'

Because Moses gave every possible reason why he could not do it, God had to use a lot of persuasion before Moses would agree, but then God said, 'When you go, I will cause Pharaoh to rebel. He will not listen to you or do what you say; he will fight against you with all his strength! I am calling you to do something which I Myself am going to make absolutely impossible! I will cause him to refuse you, and make him stronger than ever in his anger against you.

Why? So that I can then demonstrate that I am God by destroying the power of Pharaoh and delivering My people. And this will not be with human power. Instead I will demonstrate on the face of the earth the power of an Almighty God, such as has never been seen before – the greatest miracles ever seen!' Here God is dealing with the most powerful nation in the world at that time, the Egyptian Empire. The Jewish people were slaves under that system, and God had said that He would deliver the whole nation of Israel! It was impossible!

Can you understand? God chose an 80-year-old man, born into a slave family, yet brought up in the king's palace, who became a murderer, fled from the nation and spent his life as a shepherd looking after sheep in the desert! God told him, 'I have chosen YOU to go to Pharaoh and tell him to release all his slaves, empty the prison camps, set more than two million people free!' Moses protested, 'I can't do it. I'm not an ambassador, I'm not a statesman. I'm an outcast. I ran away from this nation because they were going to kill me for murder. All I have done for the past 40 years is keep sheep!'

Yet this man Moses had an experience with God. He had met God in the fire, and that fire came into HIM, transforming HIM, and now God takes the reluctant hero and commands HIM to do the impossible! This experience Moses had with God was so powerful, he could not refuse to obey. If only our encounters with God were as powerful and life-changing as this man's was! BUT after God commanded Moses, He warned him that Pharaoh would NOT listen to him and would NOT release Israel. What a shock! The only preparation for Moses was that he had met with God in the fire. Now he has a job he doesn't want, and God says, Pharaoh will NOT do what you ask! God actually says, 'I will MAKE him refuse you!' This is an amazing story. It changed my life. It's the reason why I evangelise Russia. And it can change YOUR life.

The only qualifications Moses had were the fire and the command of God. And with those two things the whole life of Moses – and the nation – was transformed!

Now, in Deuteronomy 4:32, Moses is celebrating 40 years since this greatest demonstration of God's power ever seen on earth – miracles, signs and wonders. It was enough to change the heart of Pharaoh, but why had God Himself hardened him? Why? Without Pharaoh's stubborn resistance, God could not have displayed His power, and without this, Israel would not have known the reality of who God is.

In Moses, God was demonstrating the power that is poured on, and through, the evangelist. Moses was the world's first evangelist and one of the greatest, because in one crusade he delivered two million people from the slavery of the devil and brought them into the Promised Land that God had given them. God did it the way He always does – by the impossible! But this is also a picture of the miracle that happens in the conversion of every believer.

I want to challenge you to dream the dreams of the impossible; to get a vision of the God of the impossible, who can do what no man can do. The God who has more power than any president, any army, any government, any financial corporation on the face of the earth – the God who is in control and the God who will fulfil every promise

– He will give you the command and the fire. I want you to dream until it becomes a vision and a reality. I want you to see the power and the glory of God as Moses saw it.

I have a burning ambition to live to see more of the power, more of the glory of God in this world, here, than ever seen by Moses. The miracle that defeated the power of the devil in your life – that broke the power of sin when you got saved, when God bound the power of the devil and took you from slavery and brought you into the Kingdom of God – is like the miracle Moses saw. But there is more!

Yes, Moses recalls the greatest miracle ever seen, but the prophet Jeremiah (16:14) speaks about the FUTURE, when he says that something is about to happen: 'Behold the days come, says the Lord, that it shall no more be said, the Lord lives that brought up the children out of the land of Egypt.' God says, 'There will come a day in the future when everything in the Bible will be eclipsed by the light of the miracle that I am about to do. Your past will be nothing compared with what I am going to do. Don't look at the past; look at the future!'

Let me remind you that the first miracle was the greatest demonstration of the power of God ever seen on the earth, but God says the future will be greater! Jeremiah says that the day will come when the people will forget the miracle of the deliverance from Egypt, but will say, the Lord lives, who brought the children of Israel from the land of the north – Russia!

Yes, God is saying that miracles in the future will happen in Russia, and when I look at all the prophecies over Russia, especially those of Hudson Taylor, I believe that God is going to pour out the power of the Holy Spirit there, in the greatest miracles of all time, and that I shall see it; that I shall be part of it! I believe it has already begun!

God IS once more going to show His power on earth and glorify the name of His Son by the greatest miracles ever seen! In your lifetime, in mine, by the grace of God!

I'm going to see the power of this great God in action – in Russia, now. That is why He called me to launch out to attempt the impossible. I spoke about this before I went into Russia for our great April 2004 crusades. I knew beyond doubt what God was going to do there. The first miracle would be the provision of the finance. The next was the actual satellite link-up joining seven regions of the world's largest nation in one powerful crusade with Jesus. The final one will be when the result is seen in the Kingdom, the tears of repentance and the power of God in the greatest demonstration of His power ever seen in Europe – God pouring out the Holy Spirit, working miracles greater than anything seen in the Bible. That's why, even when I see the sick healed night after night, I still go home and weep and shed tears, because this is not yet the full power of God that I am waiting to see, here on earth. Even that crusade in Russia is only the beginning.

But this move of God will only begin when men and women come again into the fire and the power of God. God can use YOU – the sinner, the outcast, born in slavery, despised, rejected – to show His power on earth!

CHAPTER THREE

THE SECRET OF POWER NOW

I like to boast about the power of my God because He is a God of action. Yes, God is a God of love, of compassion. But the God I know and serve, the God of the Bible, is not passive, but militant in action on our behalf. A God of love, but also a God of power.

Today it's time that we began to rise up and recognise the power and authority that we have in Jesus' Name. Power to preach a life-changing Gospel, power to bring healing miracles in order that He might receive the glory, and so that we as 'ordinary' people might have something dynamic to demonstrate in our lives. When Jesus healed the paralytic man (Matthew 9:6) He said, 'So that you may know that the Son of Man has power on earth . . . rise up and walk!' Today we must become men and women of action to continue the demonstration begun by Jesus, so that non-believers will desire to have what we have.

The challenge today is for believers to demonstrate who the REAL Jesus is. It's a responsibility we cannot refuse or delegate, because the people in the world are confused by religion, by all the different philosophies – we're living in a multi-cultural society and they don't know who the REAL Jesus is. Religions are merely a man-made interpretation, therefore there are many. Theology is the theory without the practice. The God I know, admire, worship and serve is a God of fire, power, action. And He requires action and obedience from us so others can find this real God.

There is a real danger that in our attempts to attract others into our faith we tend to water it down, whereas desperate people need strong faith in a strong, powerful God. So this weak Gospel repels rather than attracts those we should be winning. I believe the reason we see so many young people converted in Russia is that they are looking for a real, convincing faith, which they find, and they are converted to faith in this God of power.

Many believers are seeking a new anointing, a new power, something extra to what they already have – a Toronto Blessing, or other phenomena. I went to Jerusalem 40 years ago without receiving a new anointing. Why? What I am seeking is already within me! I have it now. I am not waiting for a new anointing. I have all the power I need in my spirit now! How? Well, 50 years ago I was seeking to be filled, baptised with the Holy Spirit. When I received, it was a manifestation of fire, of power, speaking with tongues like they did on the Day of Pentecost – and miracles soon began to follow. What a baptism of power and of fire I received that day! I received the Holy Spirit, all the mighty power of God, everything. Now that powerful anointing which before had been outside of me – that third person of the Trinity, the Holy Spirit – was now IN ME! There is only one Holy Spirit and He is in me! Not outside. I am not waiting for another Holy Spirit. He, the Spirit who raised up Jesus from the dead, who was in

Paul and Peter, that mighty, miracle-working power of the great God I am boasting about, is in me now, and He has been in me for over 50 years! I cannot receive any greater power than that I already have, in me now!

That is why I do not seek a new experience and that is why the fire has not gone out for 50 years! Yes, I am different now to what I was 50 years ago. But notice HE is not different; I am! During 50 years He has cleaned out a lot of my self and pride, my own works, and because I am not perfect, He will continue to do so until I am raptured into glory. However, He does not change. I do! Jesus said, 'He that believeth on Me, out of his inner being shall flow rivers of living water.' The Holy Spirit is the source, but the Word of God says that when we have received the Holy Spirit, the source is in us. External experiences are of the world, the flesh or the devil. The inner experience is the fresh river source, the sweet blessing, the mighty power of God, the Holy Spirit within you!

With the Gospel it is the same. The Bible says that it is 'Christ IN you, the hope of glory'. When you come to Christ and repent, you and all your old nature must die, so that you can be 'born again'. 2 Corinthians 5:17 says that if any man is in Christ he is a NEW CREATED BEING, old things are passed away, all things are new. This is why I cannot accept Christian psychology, seeking to find why we are not changed, what sin our mother committed, what trauma happened in the womb. NO. I have NO past, I am a dead man. If you believe that Jesus died on the cross, then salvation means death; you must die with Him. Colossians 2:12 says we're buried with Him in baptism and raised with Him into new life.

My old sinful life is dead – I am dead – with Christ! But

just like Jesus, I have been raised from the dead and so like Paul can say, 'I live, yet not I, Christ lives in me!' This is what I preach: the old-fashioned Gospel according to the Word of God. Every convert is a new creation. That is why REVIVAL FIRE is in Russia and the Ukraine! HE is within them and they are only alive in HIM. Dead to self, but CHRIST LIVES in US!

I have Christ IN me and I have the Holy Spirit IN me. That is the secret of 50 years of miracle ministry. I do not want any new Gospel. I want the Bible-believing, miracle-working, powerful Gospel according to God's Word! You can pray for an easy life, ask Him to prevent the problems, ask for a quiet time . . . but where there are no problems, there are no miracles!

We must go by faith, in obedience to what God is telling us to do. And God always makes a way. I have learned that everything God does is a miracle. If it's not a miracle, then you or I could do it! In my life I know that it is God working when the totally impossible happens. Whatever the problem, God never ever fails – it's impossible! The day God fails, He's no longer God. It's in God's Word, it's His character. He's the God of miracles! Yes, I have problems and these mean I spend much time in prayer and fasting. Why? Because you cannot have miracles without first having problems. Every problem drives me to prayer, which then brings another miracle! But people aren't prepared to pay the price. And because they don't want the problems, they don't see the miracles. The Bible says that the things that are impossible with men are possible with God.

For one year I spent much time in prayer and fasting, seeking an answer to a desperate need. Twice I said to the Lord that I would fast until the answer came, I was so desperate, but I know that my God is a prayer-answering God! The first time I had to cease fasting before the answer came, only because I had to go to Ukraine for three weeks of intensive evangelism. The second time was after my return: tired and exhausted from the travelling and preaching and the effects of food poisoning, I recommenced my fast, determined to continue until the answer came. After ten days, as I was praying and worshipping Him, I felt a tremendous sense of the Lord's presence and I began to say, 'Yours is the Kingdom, the power and the glory.' Suddenly it was as if this was the answer, and I began to say it again: 'Yours is the Kingdom, Yours is the power. These are Yours by right, but the GLORY is what we give You as the answer comes and You receive the glory from us!' I felt confident at that moment that without question I would receive from Him exactly what I was asking, so that then I could give Him all the glory!

'When the enemy comes in like a flood, the Spirit of the Lord raises up a standard against Him!' (Isaiah 59:19). The expression 'raising the standard' means, in military terms, going to war. So when the devil attacks, then God goes into action and you see miracles, which are the evidence of this. When you don't see the devil, you don't see any miracles either. If you sit in comfort with no problems in your life, you won't need any miracles! Do you want to see miracles? Do you want to live on the edge, in the danger zone, and see the God of power in action?

The one thing that shows strongly through the whole of the Old Testament is the way that God always gets the glory. When Israel won the battle, it was God who gave them the victory. If they lost, then it was Israel who failed, not God! God cannot fail.

CHAPTER FOUR

GOD WANTS TO FILL YOU WITH FIRE

God wants to fill you with fire, because He changes men. God wants to use you personally and I want to challenge you with this thought. When God seeks men to use today, He does not look for the ones we would look for.

In Exodus 3:2 the angel of the Lord appeared to Moses in a flame of fire in the middle of a bush. Moses was not expecting to meet with God, and he did not see Him. He simply saw a BUSH ON FIRE. If you were walking along the street, and you saw a tree on fire, you would go and look. But when Moses looked, it was not normal. The fire was in the tree, but the tree was not burnt! It was the evidence of the presence of God like burning fire.

People today say, 'I cannot see God. Where is He?' But whenever I preach the Gospel I say, 'I will PROVE to you that God is here, because God will work MIRACLES.' Unusual things like this burning bush!

God spoke to Moses out of that fire: 'I have seen the affliction of My people which are in Egypt, I've heard their cry. I know their sorrows.' So many people do not understand who God is. He is not just a great being in Heaven.

If unbelieving people try to draw pictures of God, often they liken Him to an old man with a beard. But God is not an old man, nor does He look like you. He can only be recognised by His actions! And God is not just in Heaven; He is everywhere: in Israel, in England, in America, in Bulgaria . . .

Now, how did Moses know that he was talking with God? He saw a burning tree. When I preach the Gospel, you will not see a burning tree, but you WILL see the power of God! God said to Moses, 'I have heard your prayers, I've heard your cry.' But you say, 'I don't know how to pray'. God not only hears but sees the cries of your heart. God knows your pain, God knows your weakness. God hears the person who is crippled with arthritis, the murderer in prison, the drug addict. God does not condemn, He hears their cry. He WANTS to answer with a fiery demonstration.

So God said to Moses, 'Go and find this old devil Pharaoh and tell him, "Let these people go!"' Today He calls us to say the same to the devil about the drug addicts, the alcoholics, the sinners, the criminals, the people who are hurting, the people who are in need: 'Let them go!' But Moses was afraid – like some evangelists and pastors! In Exodus 4:1 Moses answered God, 'They won't believe me, they won't listen to my voice. They will say, "You don't know God. How do we know that you have met with Him?" No, I will not go!'

God's answer to Moses was, 'What have you got in your hand?' 'Oh, that's just my wooden stick which I broke from a tree. I cut it and shaped it myself and I use it to defend the sheep from the wild animals.' Then God said to Moses, 'Throw your stick on the ground.' Immediately that stick was changed into a poisonous snake, coming straight for him, and he ran away as fast as he could!

This snake was a reality, not a picture. God understands the reality in your life. Moses was afraid and ran away from it. If there were a snake in front of me, I would run away too. But God said to Moses, 'Don't be afraid of the snake. Go and pick it up by its tail!' If you know anything about snakes, that's dangerous, because if you pick it up by its tail, it will swing round and bite you. If you're going to get it, take its head. But God said to take its tail. Why? Because God was dealing with this thing, not Moses. So Moses picked up the snake by its tail and the moment he touched it, it was no longer a snake; it was his stick again! Now Moses began to understand.

Don't be afraid, you who want to work for God. He is with you! He is going to demonstrate His presence and work miracles together in co-operation with you. That is exactly what God said to Moses. This miracle happened so that the people might believe that God appeared to Moses. You and I cannot work miracles. Only God can, and the evidence of the power of God is seen in the miracle. Only God could change that rod to a snake and, when Moses was afraid of it, change it back into a rod!

The evidence of God is in the power. When the alcoholic or the murderer comes to Christ, and when that miracle happens and his sin is forgiven, he is freed from the curse and the power of the devil and you see the power of God in his life. I'm an evangelist and I call people to repent. But for someone simply to come and repent and say, 'Oh God, I'm a miserable sinner!' is NOT a miracle. The miracle is when the curse and the power of the devil is broken. When the alcoholic, the criminal, the drug addict comes forward to repent – when his body is full of alcohol or drugs, but he is REALLY changed and goes out as an evangelist, a witness and a testimony – that change is the evidence of God, like the burning bush!

People who 'repent' every week, that's not a miracle, but CHANGED men and women ARE. The thing that excites me about the letters I receive from prisoners is that they are not complaining, 'Oh, I'm on death row.' They do not say, 'David, save my life.' They say, 'I've found trust in God through Jesus Christ. He's changed my life, and I have a home in Heaven.' THAT is the miracle, and they are preaching the Gospel in the prison!

In the natural, I have no sons. I am married with three beautiful daughters and five lovely grandchildren. But no sons. But God has worked a miracle and has given me hundreds of sons – young men whose lives have been changed by the power of God – all over the world: Russia, Siberia, Bulgaria, Ukraine. Everyone whose life is changed and will preach the Gospel with fire and with power – I am proud to call them my sons! All those whose lives are CHANGED by the power of God – God is proud to call them His sons and His daughters!

God worked the miracle with Moses' stick because Moses said, 'They will not believe.' Many people say to me, 'I don't know. How can I believe?' But when God works miracles, the miracles are the evidence of God. To Moses, the first miracle was the burning tree, then the stick that became a snake. When I preach the Gospel, you are not going to see a burning tree or a snake, but every time you will see miracles of healing – broken bones, blind eyes, cripples healed – and you will see God!

In Exodus 5, Moses eventually goes to this demon

Pharaoh and says, 'I have met with God and God has given me a message for you.' Yes, like Moses I have met with God. I know God. I have seen the fire. More than that, the fire is in me, burning in my soul. There is a power that transforms me when I preach the Gospel so that I am not the ordinary David Hathaway. I have a power – yes a fire – from God. That is why, when I declare the Word of God, miracles happen. It's not me; it's God. He wants you to know, to see the evidence of His fire and power! I know who God is and have seen Him in the burning bush.

So when Moses went to this demon Pharaoh, he said, 'I've been with God. God has spoken to me.' Pharaoh laughed at him and said in Exodus 5:2, 'Who is this God that I should obey His voice and let these people go? I do not know the Lord and I will not obey Him.' How like today this is – people saying, 'I don't know God, I will NOT listen to Him,' but these are the very ones God wants to speak to!

God does not work miracles in my ministry just for the believers. He works miracles to demonstrate the evidence to the unbelievers. You know Him. The miracles are for those who do not yet know Him. To me this is the greatest miracle.

Once, in 1994, I was preaching in a prison in Siberia and the officer in charge challenged me, 'Why are you here? You cannot change these men. I do not believe in your God. Do you understand who these men are?' In front of me were 1,400 criminals – 400 serial murderers, 200 rapists and sex offenders and 800 men even worse. I preached Christ, the Son of God that I know, who loves the sinner, and a miracle happened: 1,400 men repented. How do I know? Because some of the greatest evangelists in

Siberia today were converted on that day, in that prison. There is one, Sasha, whom I call my son. On his release he began what has become the largest prison ministry in all Russia – he has 115 ministers working under him! But it was only ten years afterwards, in 2004, that Sasha told me the real results of that one meeting in the prison in Siberia that day: 20 of those convicts are now full-time pastors! Now that is revival! So today the Gospel is going all over Siberia because those criminals are the evangelists and the preachers.

God took the ordinary stick in Moses' hand, turning it into an evil serpent. And God says to the evangelist, 'Don't run away from that serpent. Take it by the tail, pick it up, and it will become a conversion miracle.'

God says to the sinner, I have heard your cry; I have a better life for you. I've got a better way for you – if you will repent and be converted.'

CHAPTER FIVE

POSSESS THE LAND

'The Lord has given you the land! Possess it! Go in armed, ready for war!' (Deuteronomy 3:18). It is God's command, not a request, to go and take the land. I see this as a challenge in my personal life as well as in my ministry in Russia. Many ask why I see miracles of healing; why thousands repent and revival comes.

When God sent me to Russia He said, 'GO – take the land!' There is no choice – He commanded me!

What does it mean to 'possess' the land? Look at it by faith, take it by action, fight for it by power!

When I look at the promises of God, and the Bible is full of them, I want all the good things – so I have been going in and taking them! Power for miracles and healing – I'm in there, taking it! Anointing from the Holy Spirit – yes, I pray, then I go in and take it! Revival – again I go and possess the promise. I can find enough scriptures for me to believe and know that God wants revival in Russia more than I do, so in I go!

It is the same with all our lives. God has given us so many promises, it is not presumptuous to accept them by faith, then go and take them. Too many sit and wait, asking and never receiving. I remember as a boy the time when I wanted to be filled with the Holy Spirit. The old believers said, 'Wait. We must have waiting meetings.' But I am impatient and soon became tired of waiting. I said, 'Easter is coming, I will go to London to one of the big conventions and not return until I receive.' With that positive attitude I went – and received.

We must not accept the negative but emphasise the positive!

It is so easy to know what is in the Bible, but then dismiss it. We read it, study it, preach it, 'spiritualise' it, until there is a danger that we make it mean something else. But everything in the Bible can happen today. Don't limit God. I want to challenge you to a new kind of faith. We are commanded to go in and possess all the blessings which God has promised. Get into the Word of God, search for and mark in red every promise that you want in your life, then every promise you don't want, cross it out – no, NO! I want you to have the faith to go and take them ALL! I hear Christians saying they can't, but my Bible says I can do all things through Christ.

God's command to the Israelites was to go in and possess the land (Deuteronomy 3:18). His command to believers is the same. There are three things we must do:

1. Possess the spiritual blessing

We need to recognise who we are and what we are in Christ. It is important to understand the blessings God has given us. When I first realised that the promises of both the

Old and New Testament were not just for the Jews in the past and for the first disciples, but also for me as an inheritor of the same promises as a 'son of God', it opened up a whole new experience for me. While receiving my healing from throat cancer many years ago began to lead me into a more positive experience, it was the miracle which finally brought me out of a communist prison which confirmed this. It challenged my own faith that God could actually physically open my prison doors in Czechoslovakia. It happened to Paul and Silas in Philippi 2000 years ago (Acts 16), so why could it not literally happen for me today? And it did. God even used British Prime Minister Harold Wilson to make it more dramatic and provide unquestionable proof.

It is a challenge! It is easy for us as believers to read and hear about these things that happened in the Bible without personally identifying with them. But if God did these things in the past, why not believe for them today? Some Christians would dismiss miracles like speaking in tongues and healing by saying either that these were in the past, or that they were 'dispensational'; that they can only happen at certain times! The real truth is that they do not want these things to happen. It would disturb the religious 'order' of their lives.

I came into a totally new experience of faith – the realisation that if God says it, then He will always do it! This is what faith is: not faith in a promise or a healing, but faith in God as a person; that my God is a God of His Word, who will always keep a given promise! This means that you have to make a conscious decision, either to continue to live 'normally' or to live in a faith-experience of letting God's Word govern your decisions.

It is a command of God that we must possess and receive all that God has for us. It is not an option, so obey!

2. Act with faith

It takes faith to possess all that God has given and act on it. Real faith does not come easily, but it is a specific gift from God through the Holy Spirit and you can ask for it, as I do. First you must come into an experience of receiving the Holy Spirit, then you can receive His gifts. In 1 Corinthians 12 there are nine gifts. One is speaking with other tongues, but when you receive this, why not also ask for the gift of faith? If you will fight this spiritual battle, God will give a miracle, but choosing to have miracles is the hard way! Not many people have the faith to fight this battle and win. Spiritual warfare is not merely against the devil, it is also when you fight your own unbelief. My God answers prayer. If you are totally convinced, God CANNOT fail. But it takes a lot of faith to believe God to work miracles.

3. Exercise authority

Fight against the devil by taking authority over him in Jesus' Name. Command him to get out and the problem to go! Exercise the gift of faith, NOW, in a new way. This is not just receiving an answer to prayer – it means taking authority. Nobody has ever used the full amount of power that God has. There is no limit to what God can do! Elijah, Moses, David only used a small part of God's available power. No man has ever used all of God's power; not John Wesley nor Smith Wigglesworth – no one. God wants to show His power on earth, but He can only do it through you! Why not use more of His power than any man before you? When God wanted to bring His people out of Egypt, Pharaoh said no. God used Moses until Pharaoh said yes. God uses men. But only men and women willing to yield to His authority. I am not a big man with a little God. I am a little man with a big God! I may be a little David with a Goliath of a problem, but with my God I can kill him!

Take the land! Possess the promises of God. So many believers are without power because they don't understand the promises and power of God to those who believe. Don't just take 'spiritual' blessings – take the land, possess what you need in the material realm as well. When Israel went in, it meant war, a spiritual fight, but it also meant that they could have the milk and the honey, all their material needs supplied.

The greatest command is to evangelise. God pours out His Spirit for a reason – so that we can evangelise. Every revival has died out when they stopped evangelising. Possess the land! Preach the Gospel, heal the sick! God said it. Believe it. Act on it!

CHAPTER SIX

EVANGELISM BRINGS REVIVAL

I was born into revival in Britain. There are not many people alive today that have the experience of real revival in Britain that I have. Unfortunately I have also seen the revival fire die out, here in Britain and elsewhere. Every time the revival fire dies out, it is for a reason: the people have stopped praying and the churches have stopped evangelising.

My father was born in Wales, and lived there in 1904 when the great revival came. When I was a boy he told me that when the power of God fell, suddenly the churches filled and there was not enough room for the people! The churches remained open all day; as some went out others came in, so the meetings continued almost without a break. The power of the Holy Spirit was so strong that coal miners fell on their faces at the bottom of the mine, crying out to God for forgiveness. They would come out of the pit covered in coal dust and go straight into the church. When they left, the women would go in. Most people in the area would go in to pray. Many times there was no preaching – just the power of God. During that time there were no crimes, no murders, no theft – the police, the judges and the criminals were in the church together, crying out to God for forgiveness. When there was no room in the church they would even kneel in the street. Many went to the mountain to pray; at night you could see how many people were praying by the light of the candles on the slopes. The higher the lights were up the mountain, the more the power of God was in the town! If there were not so many lights – fewer praying – the power of God would be less. Revival changed the whole nation.

Over 200 years ago there was a terrible revolution in France – thousands died and France has never recovered spiritually from that revolution. Only 32 km of water separated England from the bloodshed of the French Revolution. Many believed it would come to England, which was in the grip of crime, alcoholism and deep economic crisis. But because of the preaching of two great evangelists, John and Charles Wesley, a great spiritual revival swept the whole of Britain. John Wesley travelled from town to town, village to village, preaching the Gospel all day, declaring the power and the glory of God. In fifty years he travelled 250,000 miles / 400,000 km mainly on horseback and preached 40,000 sermons. Many times he was stoned and driven out of town, BUT the power of God changed the whole nation! Secular historians say that it was only the revival that followed the preaching of the Wesleys that saved Britain from the bloodshed of the French Revolution.

We need this kind of revival today. How will it come?

As a teenager I lived in Upper Norwood on the site of Charles Spurgeon's home, near Croydon, a suburb of London. Our house was on the side of a hill and every night I would draw back my bedroom curtains, look out over the lights of the city and pray, 'O God, save the people. Send the Holy Spirit and bring revival to England. Make me an evangelist – send me!' The Acts of the Apostles is one book in the Bible which is unfinished – we are writing it now. It's the Acts of the Church, of those who believe and know Jesus, and it won't be finished until Jesus comes! We've got to know the power and the in-filling of the Holy Ghost. We've got to know the authority of Christ, and get out there and PREACH THE GOSPEL NOW!

The older I get, the more power I have, the more I become on fire! I'm more on fire now than when I was first baptised in the Holy Spirit. That's how it should be. The fire shouldn't go out; it should burn brighter! One reason the authorities in Ukraine don't like me is that everywhere I go, so many miracles happen! They don't like the miracles. They can tolerate preaching without miracles, but they know, just as in the days of the Bible, people really begin to believe when they see miracles.

There is power with God, but that power comes with an authority. When the centurion said to Jesus, 'I am a man under authority,' he meant that he received authority from above and was given authority over those below. That must be our experience. We've got the authority.

In Acts 3 Peter simply said to the crippled man, 'Such as I have give I unto you. In the Name of Jesus, get up and walk!' No long prayers, simply, 'Get up and walk!' That is the secret of powerful ministry. It's taking authority – giving what you've experienced, what you know to be real, what you know works – but you've got to have it, you've got to experience it, you've got to know it yourself. If you haven't got it, get it!

Today so much emphasis in ministry in the church is on what God can do for us. So often we're wanting to receive things from Him just for ourselves. I remember American President John Kennedy's famous words at his inauguration: 'I don't count what my country can do for me, but what I can do for my country.' As active believers we need to say the same. Not 'What is God going to do for me?' but 'What am I going to do for God?'

You need to know what God wants in your life! You may say, 'How can I know what He wants? I keep asking Him, but I don't get any answers.' But with a married couple, the wife doesn't have to ask the husband every day, 'What do you want?' If there is the right relationship between them, the wife KNOWS what the husband wants and the husband KNOWS what the wife wants. You begin to think alike, you want the same things, you do the same things, you go to the same places. When you know God, when you have a close relationship with Him, you don't have to be always asking, 'O God, what do You want? Do I do this? Or that?' If you have the Holy Spirit within you, you will KNOW the mind and the will of God! Romans 8 says, 'When we know not what to pray for as we ought, He that knows the mind of God makes intercession for us with groanings which cannot be uttered.' When you really know Him, when you live with Him, when you walk every day in the Spirit, you KNOW what God wants! Preach the Gospel, evangelise! There is only one great commission in the Bible: 'Preach the Gospel, heal the sick!' That is the way to revival.

Do you know what God wants? He wants His glory to be seen in the whole world. He wants to use YOU as the demonstration of His power to the whole world. God wants to see fire in YOU That is why He sent the Holy Spirit to revive YOU. The church should not be cold and dead, but on fire! Receive the Holy Spirit NOW. If you are already baptised in the Spirit, do as I do and ask for another Pentecost NOW; ask for a baptism of FIRE!

Years ago a pastor invited a local businessman to come to his church. Even though he asked him many times, he never came. One night the pastor was roused from his bed because the church was burning, and because it was on a hill, crowds gathered to watch. As the pastor approached, he saw this businessman at the front of the crowd and shouted to him, 'It's too late now. Why didn't you come before?' The businessman replied, 'Because I've never seen your church on fire before!'

Revival will come when we do two things

FIRST, don't let go of God. Cry out to Him in prayer, day and night! THEN go out and preach the Gospel! This is the challenge.

Everywhere where I see revival in the world today, I see evangelism in the fire of the Holy Spirit – this is the evidence – and everywhere I see evangelism in the fire of the Holy Spirit, I see revival! We need God's FIRE! Our God is a God of power and of glory, and the Bible says His glory must be seen from one side of the world to the other. God is waiting to demonstrate His salvation to the unbelievers by reviving YOU!

CHAPTER SEVEN

REAL EVANGELISM

'The Gospel of Christ is the power of God' (Romans 1:16). Evangelism should be part of our spiritual walk with God. If I ask you what are the essentials for every Christian, especially new converts, to do, you would quickly tell me: pray every day, read the Word every day, join a real live church. Water baptism and so on would quickly follow, along with serving God, fellowship with the saints and of course to be filled with the Spirit. I would add to this evangelise, but not the way so many think of evangelism or evangelists. The Gospel is simply the good news. Your first responsibility after conversion is to spread the wonderful news of what God has done for you!

If God has saved you from your sin, believe me, that is a big miracle. You were some real kind of sinner, and for God to forgive YOU was one of the biggest miracles of all time. Sin is far more potent than the worst sickness on earth. Sickness can cripple the body and I have love and concern for those who are sick. That is why I have such compassion to heal the sick by the power of God. Many sicknesses, like cancer and heart disease, will bring death, but sin has already destroyed the soul. Every sinner is dead – to God. To bring a sinner from hell to Heaven is like bringing the dead back to life. Every born-again believer is literally one born from the dead. The only way to get rid of sin is to die. 'The soul that sins must die' (Ezekiel 18:20). That is God's command and the verdict of God's judgement. That judgement cannot be changed – or God is not consistent and becomes a liar! But Christ died not for the righteous but for the very sinner worthy only of death in God's eyes (Romans 5:6). So Jesus Christ died in your place, took your punishment – death – to bear the wrath and judgement of God in your place, so that you can live! You do not need to die. You can live, but only if your personal sin is on Jesus. How can this be? Jesus said, 'Except a man be born again, he cannot see the Kingdom of God' (John 3:3), and, 'God sent His Son that whosoever believes in Him shall not die' (John 3:16).

Suddenly we all become self-righteous, and begin to compare ourselves with others: 'His sin is bigger than mine. I'm better than some of those in my church. Look what they do. I would never do that, and yet they profess to be Christians!' Forget it. You are deluding yourself. God has said that if you break one law you are guilty of breaking them all (James 2:10). Curse your brother and it is as if you murdered him (Matthew 5:22). A lie is the same as murder! Scripture also says that all have sinned (Romans 3:23).

Therefore if you have total, absolute forgiveness from sin – if you have died the death and been born again – then this is the biggest miracle of all time. You have been raised from the dead, and the Bible says it clearly: 'For if we have been planted together in the likeness of His death, we shall be in the likeness of His resurrection' (Romans 6:5).

That is why I am an evangelist – because my own salvation is a miracle bigger than any other. Because I committed one sin I am guilty of all sin; one lie, and I cannot condemn the murderer. So if God can forgive me, He can forgive everyone! I know how deeply sin offends God, and how serious are the sins of some of the KGB who have come to me. Look at the guilt of Slobodan Milosovic, who has ordered the ethnic cleansing of thousands in Kosovo. Spiritually they are dead before God. But so was I – my sin made me dead to God!

You know that I see thousands of healings – probably very few people alive today have seen the vast numbers of healings that I have witnessed. Day after day – cripples running, broken limbs mended; those born blind seeing, those blinded by accidents, new eyes instantly created; cancers disappearing – and all these happening instantaneously. But the miracle of my own salvation from sin is a thousand times bigger than any miracle I have witnessed. I have seen storms stilled, aircraft appear miraculously, men opposing me die by the hand of God. I have been in peril in the air, tortured in prison, beaten and left for dead, seen miracles in Siberia. But my salvation is the biggest miracle I have ever seen.

However, even though I am an evangelist I have not yet raised anyone from the dead, though I am still expecting this. But I have been raised from death to life! Yes, I have been healed from cancer, miraculously released from a ten-year prison sentence in Czechoslovakia. BUT no miracle I have ever seen, heard about or dreamed about can equal the miracle of my salvation and I will shout until the whole earth can hear that only God could do this. That is what evangelism is: shouting about God's power in MY life. Forget all about the preaching, the Bible schools, the homiletics. The reality is mine and I am determined to tell the whole world by every possible means – radio, TV, books, tapes, in the street or in the stadiums. I don't need diplomas or certificates to testify; just the joy of knowing that a miracle happened in MY life and I want YOU to know. Because God can do the same for you.

People get healed and everybody wants to know – they go and testify that God worked a miracle. But IF you have my kind of salvation, you have the biggest miracle of all. Tell everyone. If you don't, I question the certainty of your personal salvation. Perhaps you had better get on your knees right now and cry out to God, 'I want to know I have forgiveness from sin, deliverance from the devil, from death and all demon power. Let it burn into my soul like a fire of glory until I too can shout hallelujah! I want to know that I'm saved by God's mighty power from death and hell! I want this to be like a Holy Ghost fire burning in my heart. Amen!' Now if it is real, get up from your knees, experience the joy and the power, tell the world – and you ARE an evangelist!

The miracle is that Jesus died, then rose again and now He cannot die ever again. He is immortal. I am the same! I died with Christ and rose again, but in my case spiritually rather than physically. Therefore I am immortal and cannot die. Not yet in the physical sense, but spiritually, until the return of Christ!

This is the importance of water baptism, which the Bible says is symbolic of this death and resurrection (Romans 6:3–5).

The only difference between you and me is that I

KNOW only GOD could save me, and HE DID! That is all it takes to be an evangelist! If you are not an evangelist, then you're uncertain of what has happened in your life. Get certain now! Jesus is coming!

When Jesus healed the ten lepers, only one returned to give thanks and He said, 'Where are the other nine?' Is it true that out of ten converts only one returns to be an evangelist? How can you give thanks to God for your salvation without testifying publicly? When I was a young man working in a bank in the City of London, I made a covenant with God not to let one day pass without witnessing about Jesus. I spent my weekends giving out tracts. I didn't want to go to Bible college because I believed that Jesus is coming and time was too short – I wanted to tell everyone. Shortly after entering the college they gave me a small church to pastor as well as studying! I was the only student in Bible college with a church! When the summer vacation came, I borrowed a tent and put it in a field to preach the Gospel. After I left college I pastored a church, but I kept going away to evangelise and plant more churches. I did not go to Russia to become an evangelist. I went to Russia because I already was one!

CHAPTER EIGHT

WHO IS THE REAL JESUS?

Matthew 8:23–27 says, 'Jesus entered into a ship . . . and behold there arose a great storm in the sea, so much that the ship was covered with the waves, but Jesus was asleep. His disciples woke Him, saying, 'Lord, save us, we're going to die!' And He said, 'Why are you so afraid, O you of little faith?' Then He arose and rebuked the winds and the sea and there was a great calm. The men marvelled, and said, 'What kind of Man is this?''

That's the challenge! The world is looking for a man, a leader to follow. They'll follow corrupt politicians, even Hitler or Stalin, and one day the Antichrist. But what kind of Man is this in the Bible? Don't despise the Bible. This book changes men, destroys demons, breaks the curse of evil, gives life to the dead and healing to the sick. It's the power of God in today's world. It's the Word of the living God.

In this story, Jesus was asleep. A storm arose, so the disciples woke Him saying, 'We're all going to die! It's the end of the world . . . ' But Jesus just got up, bound the storm, the winds stopped, the boat was safe, nobody died – and when those strong fishermen saw the demonstration of the power that this Man had over the elements, they said, 'What kind of Man do we have in the boat?'

Anyone who has witnessed the real acts of God's power in the twentieth/ twenty-first century must ask the same question: What kind of Man is this?

The disciples thought He was asleep. The world today thinks He is merely a figure in history. But today Jesus is not a babe in His mother's arms – He is a God of power, of action, of authority. He's a Man real men can admire and follow. In churches I see images of Jesus as a powerless dead man on a cross. I know Jesus died, but everybody dies. Lenin, Stalin, Hitler all died, and one day, unless Jesus comes first, you will die too. But the difference is that when they put Jesus in a grave, it couldn't hold Him. The power of the Holy Spirit came into His dead body, He broke open that grave and He came out. He's alive! What kind of Man is this? The grave cannot hold Him, the wind and the sea are obedient to Him, no demon spirit in hell can stand against Him, no human can resist Him! That's the kind of God that I have!

I often have to come against the devil. In 1998, I was in a town in Siberia called Magnitogorsk, preaching in a packed auditorium. I called the people to repent, then called the sick. One 43-year-old man came. As a boy of 17, he broke his back – not once, but twice. This man was crippled for life – the doctors couldn't heal him. He was certified as an invalid of the first category, he had a state pension and could never work. In the beginning he was bedridden. Now he had learnt to walk with crutches, but for 15 to 20 days every month he was still totally bedridden. For 26 years the pain never left him. Now he came forward, and this same Jesus of the Bible was there! I looked at this 43-year-old crippled man and put my hand on him saying, 'I believe God is good. The devil is bad – broken backs don't come from God. The Bible says: "For this purpose was the Son of God revealed, to destroy the works of the devil!" (1 John 3:8). Be healed in Jesus' Name!'

I like people to demonstrate their healing, so I asked him to bend down. He refused. In his own words later he said, 'I don't know what happened – it must have been the Holy Spirit – but suddenly I found myself going over backwards in a bridge until my hands touched the ground! I had never done this before!' That's how great that miracle was.

The next night he came to tell everybody what God had done. There were some Satanists present and this man called them forward. 'You believe in the devil. Feel this big lump on my back. That's what your master the devil did to me 26 years ago!' Then suddenly he threw himself backwards, demonstrating his healing, then turned to the Satanists, 'That's what my Master Jesus did!' Those Satanists repented because they saw the power of God! That's right! God loves the sinners. Jesus said, 'I didn't come to call the good, the righteous, the religious.' He came to call the Satanists, Neo-Nazis, drug addicts, alcoholics . . .

Eighteen months later we were back in the same town. Vladimir was the first to greet me. He's brought many people to faith in Christ through his testimony, and he's also got married since he was healed!

The disciples in the boat marvelled at Jesus – they didn't realise they had this kind of Man in the boat. They were astonished. What kind of Man is this? He's got so much power – not just women and children but the wind and the waves obey Him! He is the Lord of Heaven and earth, the Jesus who still works miracles today. He is the Son of the living God! And He's my Jesus! He's real!

The first time I preached in Susuman, Siberia, in 1994, I only had two days in the stadium. On the first night the power of God came down and miracles started to happen. One woman came out of the hospital and God instantly healed her crippled legs. She asked me to come into the hospital with her next day. The Holy Spirit said, 'Go!' Next morning she ran up four flights of stairs and took me into a men's ward. I laid hands on the first man in Jesus' Name, and his broken back was instantly healed and he got out of bed! The second man also had a broken back and he was instantly healed. The third man had lost his sight. In Jesus' Name I rebuked the power of the devil. I gave him my interpreter's Russian Bible and he began to read it. He was so excited, he ran all over the hospital, shouting, 'It's a miracle! I can see! Look, I'm reading the Bible!' – and he read the Word of God to the whole hospital! It was the demonstration of the power of Jesus through that blind man. The news spread and that night so many people came into the stadium, a quarter of the town repented in two days! That whole town was stirred by the power of God in a way I had never ever seen before in my life.

After I left, the priest cursed the people who were healed; he cursed the whole town. The next year I was asked back. The priest came into the meeting to curse me and the people, saying, 'I will drive you out of town with whips. I will denounce you on television.' So I went to the television first! They gave me 30 minutes to speak. Under the anointing of the Holy Spirit, I told the whole town that God loves them and I called them to repent. The entire message was shown on the main TV channel that night immediately before the international news! But because of the priest we could not use the auditorium that night. We had to preach in the street and we put our loudspeakers around Lenin's statue! The priest sent a male witch, who called evil spirits to destroy the meeting. He summoned an electric storm – these men have power – and a great wind came and big drops of rain started to fall. I went straight up to that man and bound the power of the devil in him. My Jesus is Lord! There was a flash of lightning direct on the man. He fell to the ground, then ran down the street – and the rain followed him against the wind! I have never seen such a thing in my life before. Jesus has power over the wind and the rain, and not just in Galilee! Now today in that town there's a good pastor, a strong church. They're on fire, and they're training evangelists to win Russia for Christ!

We need to demonstrate the power and reality of the Gospel. We're so far through prophecy, we don't have time just for words; we need to see action! Let me challenge you: what kind of Man is this Jesus? Wherever I go, He's in the boat! I'd rather be in a 'storm' with Jesus than living in calm and peace without Him. I want you to know this real Jesus in your life. Most of us, even as believers, experience some powerful storms in our lives. That is why we need the reality of the Man who can conquer them!

CHAPTER NINE

I WILL NOT COMPROMISE . . .

'Jesus Christ, made of the seed of David according to the flesh, and declared to be the Son of God with power, according to the Spirit of holiness, by the resurrection from the dead' (Romans 1:3–4). Paul says that Jesus is set apart, because He is declared to be the Son of God with POWER. Very clearly in Scripture, Jesus Christ is confirmed to be the Son of God by the demonstration of power in His life. In the Acts 2:22, Peter speaks in the same way: 'Jesus of Nazareth, a man' – emphasising God as man – 'approved of God among you by miracles, by wonders, by signs.'

The church of today is apologetic

Formal Christianity has totally moved away from the miraculous, and the moment that you do, you've lost the purpose of our Christian faith and its power. If there were no miracles in the life of Jesus – the virgin birth, the resurrection and the miracles of His ministry – then He is no different from any other so-called god or prophet. In India they have thousands of gods. How do you know which one is the right one? Today we are being told that there are many faiths. In Britain, according to our parliamentary broadcasting act, we are not supposed (for fear of infringing the rights of, or offending, others) to say publicly on TV that there is only one way of salvation. But there IS only one way! Only ONE God. I will NOT compromise.

I want you to understand the importance of miracles to the ministry

Peter, on the Day of Pentecost, talking about Jesus, says, 'You yourselves know the man, born in Nazareth, His father, His mother, His brothers and sisters. But we know He was different because God demonstrated it by miracles, by signs, by wonders!' That is the Word of God and I believe everything in the Word of God is true. Either believe it all, or don't believe any of it! If you start to take bits out of the Bible, what have you left? Even in the Old Testament, how did God deliver Israel out of Egypt? By miracles. How did God cause Israel to repent when they were worshipping Baal in the time of Elijah? By a miracle of fire.

If you ask Moslems about Jesus, they will willingly talk about Him. They don't deny Jesus. They accept that He's an historical figure, referred to in the Koran; that He's the son of Mary. But they say He was only a prophet, not the Son of God. Moslems say that God has no Son. It's written inside their mosques and in the Dome of the Rock in Jerusalem: 'Jesus, Son of Mary, is only an apostle of God . . . God is only one God. Far be it from His glory that He should have a Son.' So to them Jesus was a prophet, but

Mohammed was greater. But many Moslems are more dedicated, stricter in their observance of their religion, than Christians are!

What IS the difference between Jesus and Mohammed?

Very simple: Mohammed was not the son of God. He wasn't even a prophet. He was an illiterate political leader who generated a religion around himself in order to persuade his followers. Our Jesus is the Son of the living God. How do we know? Because God confirmed it by the miracles. This is what makes Jesus different. And the biggest miracle of all? When they put Him to death, on the third day God raised Him from the dead! Jesus is alive TODAY; Mohammed is dead. He will only rise on the Judgement Day for condemnation. Therefore we have a more effective and powerful faith than any Moslem, and we should be more active than them in declaring who our Jesus is!

Practical Faith

We need the power of the Holy Spirit to see miracles. There are nine gifts of the Holy Spirit mentioned in 1 Corinthians 12: three vocal gifts – speaking with tongues, the interpretation of tongues, and prophecy; three intellectual gifts – the word of knowledge, the word of wisdom and the discerning of spirits; three practical gifts – the gift of healing, the working of miracles and the gift of faith. The gift of faith is NOT an intellectual gift. If you see faith as only an intellectual gift, you will never see its power. It is a practical gift. It's the one I ask for more than any other gift.

Jesus HEALED the sick

Jesus never once in the four Gospels told His disciples to pray for the sick. He said, 'HEAL the sick!' (Luke 9 and 10). He was speaking with authority. This isn't a game you play. He said you've got authority to preach the Gospel and HEAL the sick – both are the command of Christ. Yes, in James 5:14 it says that the prayer of faith will save the sick, but this is in the church. There is a big difference between the call of the evangelist and ministry within the church. 'Preach the Gospel; HEAL the sick!' As an evangelist, I HAVE to do it. It's a command. I CAN'T stop preaching the Gospel, I CAN'T stop healing miracles following. And God will even heal the unbelievers – whether they repent or not!

The first time I began major evangelism in Siberia in 1994, I took 400 co-evangelists and spent three months there, 16,000 km away from home. We didn't have enough money when we went and I had just enough for one-way tickets. Some asked me where the return tickets were, and I told them, 'In the Gospels Jesus said "Go" many times – He never once said, "Come back!"' But God did provide and we came back – by faith!

One newspaper in England investigated whether I had actually been to Siberia! They printed a whole page article. Yes, David Hathaway did go for three months and the organisation was good. Yes, there were many miracles of healing and everyone they had spoken to who had claimed healing was indeed still healed. But they criticised, because they said that not all those healed were in the churches!

But in the Gospels, how many men followed Jesus? He fed 5000 men plus women and children and I'm sure that sometimes He preached to more than 20,000. How many did He heal? Take one example – ten lepers, only one returned. Maybe in Jerusalem when the crowds were crying out, 'Crucify Him!' there were some among them who had been healed. And if there were some who hadn't been healed, they would have been shouting louder still. Only a few of those thousands who had followed Jesus and been healed remained loyal to Him at the end. We face the same situation today. But I want to make it absolutely clear: I cannot find anywhere in the New Testament where Jesus differentiated and said, 'You're a believer, so you'll get healed,' and 'You're not a believer, so I'm sorry, I won't heal you.' Matthew 8:16 says, 'He healed all.'

In Matthew 9:6, Jesus healed the paralytic 'so that you may know that the Son of Man has power on earth to forgive sins'.

Authority

For me the most important chapter in the Bible on healing is Matthew 8. Jesus came down from the mountain and thousands followed Him. A leper came and said, 'If you want to, You can heal me!' Jesus said, 'I want to!' and it was done. Then Jesus came into Capernaum and a Roman centurion came to Him: 'Lord, I have a sick servant at home.' Jesus said, 'I'll come to your house.' The centurion replied, 'Don't, I'm not a good man,' and I don't suppose he was if he was a Roman centurion! But the officer said the most amazing thing: 'One word from You and my servant will be healed! I'm a man under authority, an officer in the most powerful army in the world. I have authority from those above, and over those under me. My men obey me. Jesus,

I recognise in You the same authority.'

Yes, I have an anointing, but I also have an authority, direct from God, over the devil, over sickness, over sin. Jesus did not heal the sick by His praying. He healed them by His authority, by His word of command. With this centurion, Jesus spoke the word and the centurion believed, went home and his servant was healed.

In verse 16, when the evening was come, they brought Him many who were possessed with devils, and he cast out the spirits with His word. And He healed all who were sick, probably including the sceptics and unbelievers. Jesus healed to demonstrate His authority, not just to test the faith or spiritual level of the cripples. When I minister, I do not actually pray for the sick, but I command the sickness to go. My praying comes first before I even start to minister. I need to fast and pray to receive the faith that comes through the Holy Spirit and to receive my authority for the healing miracles that follow.

I take my authority directly from God and from His Word. This is what the Roman officer understood; that Jesus was a man like himself who had been given authority. The centurion's authority was over men; Jesus' authority was over the devil, sin and sickness. We need to understand that we can also receive this authority in our own lives, if we live by faith and obedience to His authority.

I stand on the authority and the Word of God. Jesus is set apart, because He is declared to be the Son of God with POWER. God demonstrates this TODAY by miracles, by signs, by wonders. I will NOT compromise.

CHAPTER TEN

WHY GET EXCITED?

'Whosoever shall call upon the Name of the Lord shall be saved. But how shall they call on Him in whom they've not believed? Or believe in Him of whom they have not heard? Or hear without a preacher?' (Romans 10:13). The evangelist is the preacher, the witness, the testimony to the power of God. As an evangelist I believe in telling everybody about Jesus because I believe in Him. He's real! He's alive! There is nobody like Him in all the world! And He's going to come back to the earth very soon! Isn't He wonderful! Real believers should be the happiest people on earth. Religion gives you complicated rules which can put you in bondage, but faith in Christ sets you free from the law, and the power of sin and death.

My God is wonderful and I want to boast about Him – A GOD WHO IS ALIVE AND CHANGES MEN AND WORKS POWERFUL MIRACLES!

During February 1998, while evangelising in Siberia, I became excited because one night a man gave his testimony. He had stolen from a shop and been put in prison, but in the prison he lost his temper and killed a man, ending up with a 21-year sentence! Four years ago, while still there, somebody told him about Jesus Christ. He believed, repented and began to serve Jesus. Now he had only been out of prison two months and yet already he had won his whole family to Christ, was evangelising every day, and he was the happiest man in the meeting that night. What had happened? He had felt the power of God come into his life. He did not become religious, but he really believed and this faith changed him. His happiness was a demonstration of the real change in his life – not his release from prison, but his release from the guilt of murder!

I want you to get as excited as I am about who the REAL Jesus is. Being a believer longer than most of you, I've experienced many problems, such as cancer, and have spent a year in prison for the Gospel – but in all my life GOD HAS NEVER FAILED ME ONCE. He has ALWAYS answered my prayers. There is no one like Him. If you knew MY Jesus, you would become so enthusiastic, so full of the power of the Holy Spirit, that the whole world would want to know YOUR Jesus. Enthusiasm is extremely infectious. I've been a salesman, so I know that people aren't stupid. They quickly know if you really believe in what you are selling!

While speaking in Australia I saw a lot of miracles of healing. Michelle, 22 years old and born crippled with a curved spine, was instantly healed, and not only straightened, but grew more than four inches in height! Then there was Naomi, 25 years old. As a child of eight she had accidentally poked a knitting needle through her right eye, blinding herself. When I laid my hands on her a creative miracle happened and she could read small print with the blind eye! And there was Natasha. Victim of a hit-and-run accident one year previously, the vertebrae in her spine had been crushed and the nerves in her left leg destroyed. She lay on the floor the whole meeting. I put my hands on her in Jesus' Name, then, to test, I asked her sister to tickle her foot. Natasha began to laugh, rolled over and jumped to her feet completely healed!

The TV became interested and sent a camera crew to interview me, saying that they would show just 60 seconds on the news. The girl reporter became so excited at the simple reality of Jesus that she was in tears, ready to repent. The TV then went on to interview some of those miraculously healed and to make a full documentary!

Some find it difficult to accept miracles and healings. They want the Gospel without. Let me ask you a question. Which is the bigger miracle: to see an alcoholic, drug addict or murderer instantly forgiven and delivered, or to see a broken leg instantly healed, a blind person reading the Bible and a paralytic getting out of a wheelchair? How can you really believe in an instant conversion and yet not an instant healing without limiting God's power?

While I was holding crusades in Russia, in October 1998, a man who had been badly burned came into one of the meetings. Three months before, a container of boiling tar had exploded, the tar engulfing his legs. He stood in front of me still in agony. This was Russia and it had taken too long to get to hospital. Even then, the lack of medical equipment and supplies meant that little had been done to help him. What a challenge! What can your God do for such an extreme case? He told us that to remove the tar, they had 'cut the meat off his legs'. I just reached out and touched his pain-racked body, saying, 'In the Name of Jesus, I command the pain and injury to go!' That's all, but immediately the pain went! He came back the next night to say that the pain had not returned. He had slept for the first time in three months and the 'meat was growing back on his legs'. He was so excited, he grabbed the microphone and told everyone, 'It's real! This Jesus is real! My legs are a miracle! This is not religion or psychology. Jesus is the real thing!' I could have wept for joy – with this kind of miracle the world would believe on Him! No wonder when God sent Jesus into the world it was the miracles He used to convince the unbelieving Jews! This is why I get so excited. I don't just 'believe'; I KNOW Jesus!

Often in a crowd of several thousand people I tell them that my God is alive and will work miracles NOW! However, this takes not only faith, but courage. In one crusade in a football stadium in Kherson, a large city in southern Ukraine, there was little faith in the thousands of unbelievers in the crowd. What could I do to prove that the God of the Bible is alive and has power and can work miracles today? I had called the people to repent and thousands had responded, but it now needed a big demonstration to prove the truth of God's Word. I asked for only people with broken arms and legs to come to the platform. Eleven came forward, every one with broken bones. This was not easy. I could only do it because I was under a powerful anointing from the Holy Spirit. If I was wrong, how could I continue the crusade? I would be laughed at. But I know HIM, and surprisingly, God loves a challenge! God loved it when David challenged Goliath, when Elijah called down fire on Mount Carmel. God is not afraid. I laid my hands on all eleven. What does the Bible say in Mark 16? These signs will follow those who believe. They will put their hands on the eleven people with broken arms and legs . . .

and what will happen? They will be healed! I know what the Bible says, I know God has the power and I know HIM!

I asked the Holy Spirit to work a miracle and exalt the Name of Jesus so that everyone in the stadium would know that this was not me but the Lord Himself. I became excited because HE HEALED THEM ALL – instantly, in front of the crowd, just as it was in Jesus' day and just like the Acts of the Apostles, only it happened HERE and NOW! Not past but present, not abstract but reality, not words but actions! This is why I speak with confidence. As the apostle said, 'I KNOW in whom I have believed!'

On another occasion I knew in my spirit that the people did not really believe, so when one woman in the crowd came for healing, I looked at her and asked, 'Do you believe?' and she said, 'Oh, I believe, I believe!' But I knew she didn't, so I asked her, 'What do you believe?' She was shocked because I questioned her. She said, 'I believe everything!' That meant she believed in flying saucers, religion, witchcraft and even the devil, but she did not know God!

This is the real problem: people don't KNOW God! In Romans 10:13 it says that, whosoever shall call upon the Name of the Lord shall be saved, but how can they call on a God they do not BELIEVE in?

That woman I was talking to was religious, but didn't really believe. 'Having religion' doesn't make you a believer. There is only ONE WAY you can REALLY believe. It's if you KNOW WHO GOD IS. You can learn every word in the Bible – you can know everything about religion – but if you don't know God, it means ABSOLUTELY NOTHING. Faith is more than knowing the Bible; it is knowing THE GOD OF THE BIBLE,

HAVING A PERSONAL RELATIONSHIP WITH HIM.

If you could know Jesus like this, absolutely nothing is impossible. My Jesus heals the sick, mends broken bones and specialises in the things no human doctor can do. That prisoner in Siberia – who else could forgive his sin and change his life? What an exciting God! A God of miracles, a God of power and authority! A God who changes people's lives! I want you to experience His forgiveness as you come to Him now. Approach Him personally as a friend! But ask His forgiveness for all your sin, then accept it by faith . . . in Him alone!

Now what God is calling you to do is to demonstrate that your sin is forgiven and that you know Him. Now you can preach the Gospel and tell the whole world how wonderful Jesus is. Boast about Him! Tell them He's real! Get excited, share your enthusiasm!

This is why I preach the Gospel today, all over the world, and I don't have time for anything else: He is the most important thing in my life.

God is not going to evangelise the world – nor is He sending Jesus back to do it. YOU are! In Acts 1 Jesus said to His disciples, 'After the Holy Spirit has come upon you, YOU will receive POWER and YOU will be MY WITNESSES.' If you believe, ALL the power that is in Heaven is in YOU, but YOU have to go out and DO IT!

CHAPTER ELEVEN

WATER BAPTISM IS A DEMONSTRATION OF FAITH

'He that believes and is baptised will be saved, but whoever does not believe will be damned' (Mark 16:16). The Scripture is clear: we are saved by faith.

On the Day of Pentecost, when Peter preached Christ crucified and risen from the dead, there was such conviction that the crowd asked him, 'What shall we do?' He answered, 'Repent and be baptised' (Acts 2:37–38). To do this certainly requires faith. True repentance is not only being sorry for sin (fear of punishment when we are found out can bring this). It means being sorry enough to leave our sin. This can only happen when we are convicted by the Holy Spirit of what sin is and how our sin grieves God. We then come to faith in Christ, believing that by His death our sin is cancelled. This is confirmed by the episode in Philippi where at midnight, as a result of Paul and Silas praying and praising God, an earthquake burst open their prison. The effect on the jailer of this miraculous sign was to bring him under conviction of his own sin by the power of the Holy Spirit until he asked, 'What must I do to be saved?' (Acts 16:30). To me this is wonderful, to have someone so under conviction that THEY ask the question. Pray that this will happen in Russia, in the UK, in your country, by the Holy Spirit! Paul answered, 'Believe (have faith) on the Lord Jesus.' And immediately he was baptised (verses 31–33), strong biblical evidence as to why baptism in water must follow as part of our salvation.

Why water?

First let us examine what this baptism in water symbolises. Literally it means to be buried, as when you die. Look at Colossians 2:12 – buried with Christ in baptism and raised with Him through your faith. This is clearly symbolic of the death of all your past life, buried in the water. Then as Christ Jesus rose from the grave and from death, so we are to rise with Him, 'through faith', out of the water. It was the same extraordinary step of faith for Jesus, who died in absolute belief that He would be raised in three days. Our baptism must be a demonstration of the same faith.

Tradition or Scripture?

There are conflicting traditions in the church. One is of infant baptism by sprinkling. This cannot fulfil Acts 2:38, which requires repentance first. How can a baby or even a child without a knowledge of sin repent? In addition it is significant to look at Matthew 3. When John was unwilling to baptise Jesus, He rebuked him, saying, 'Thus it becomes us to fulfil all righteousness.' Immediately after, we find that both of them went into the River Jordan, confirming by implication, and by the actual word used, that Jesus was not sprinkled but rather immersed. The Bible shows that our baptism in water symbolises death. How can sprinkling do this?

The Orthodox

In the ninth century, two brothers, Kiril and Metodi, Greek Orthodox believers, were sent to convert the Slavic tribes. The Church commissioned them to translate the Bible into Slavic. As there was no written form of the language and no biblical terminology, they constructed the language we know as Russian, creating and using Kyrilic (Cyrillic) script. There are a number of interesting results. One is that the word used for the first day of the week, Sunday, literally means 'resurrection'! So throughout the 72 years of communist/atheistic domination, not even the biggest sinner could forget the miracle that Jesus is alive, and that there IS a resurrection – even for the damned! Unfortunately there are more than 400 mistranslations in the Russian Bible (let me qualify this by saying that these are words which differ in translation from the truth which we accept as in the King James version). When Kyril and Metodi translated the Bible from the original Greek into the pagan Slavic language, they had to 'create' some new words to cover concepts that did not exist in the Slavic. Based on 'Christ', their word for the cross is 'krest'. And made up from this word is 'kresteet', to baptise, and 'kresteetsia', to make the sign of the cross (not found in the Bible but used in religious tradition). 'Perekresteet' in Russian means both to christen (baptise) and to make the sign of the cross. This means that in the Russian, 'He that believes and is baptised shall be saved' (Mark 16:16) is easily understood as 'He that crosses himself shall be saved'!

In the Orthodox tradition, the priest makes the sign of the cross over the baptismal water, the candidate for baptism (infant or adult) is sprinkled with water, and the sign of the cross (using a specially dedicated oil) is made on the forehead, the eyes, the nostrils, the mouth, the ears, the heart, the hands and the feet. Small wonder that the Orthodox Christian is fully persuaded that it is the sign of the cross made over him by the priest that saves him, and that he also continually 'crosses' himself – as he is taught to do. Wearing a cross round the neck is a popular religious/superstitious tradition worldwide, and many unbelieving people in the West do this.

Today, in Russia and Ukraine, older traditionalists coming forward for salvation or healing will immediately cross themselves, believing that it is a necessary part of their religion. This is NOT a part of our salvation, nor is it found in the original Greek in which the New Testament was written. Anything other than this has come only from traditions and doctrines which have been introduced into the church by men, not by inspiration of the Holy Spirit, who does not contradict the Word of God. Only obedience to the command of God can give full assurance of salvation.

In Western tradition

In the first centuries after Christ, when the Roman Empire was thoroughly pagan and bitterly persecuted the church, the importance of faith in Christ was fully understood. The sign or symbol of the cross was not used.

By the end of the third century AD, the Roman Empire was consumed by civil war. Then, in AD 312, Constantine, ambitious to seize control of the empire, engaged in battle against his rival Maxentius, at Milvian Bridge, Italy. It is said that in a dream or a vision before the battle, Constantine saw the sign of the cross in the sky and the words, 'In this sign shall you conquer!' He went into battle with the sign of the cross hurriedly painted on the shields of his soldiers, and he won a resounding victory – so effectively that he held the reins of power in the empire for 25 years.

Superstition?

The power of the Christian God had, it clearly seemed to Constantine, triumphed over the pagan magic of his enemy. He ended state persecution against the church, and history records him as the first 'Christian' Emperor. But we can wonder about that. Yes, he ended Emperor worship, but he kept the traditional title of Chief Priest of the pagan state religion, taking a strong interest in the regulation of both the Christian and pagan religions, giving equal rights to all.

Was this 'faith' or was it superstition in the sign of the cross by which he was 'saved' and by which he conquered? It is known that Constantine was not baptised until his deathbed, out of fear that his post-baptismal sins would not be forgiven. It is also known that his mother, Queen Helena, introduced into the church the veneration of holy places, relics and statues – a dead pagan substitute for living faith in God.

It is from this time on that the sign of the cross became so important in religious ceremonies. When later the empire divided into east and west, the sign of the cross was firmly entrenched both in Orthodox traditions in the East and Catholic traditions in the West.

The Israelites

It is interesting to see there is another symbolism in water baptism (1 Corinthians 10:2). When the Israelites came out of Egypt to worship God, they were led not by the easy way but by the strategically planned hard way, through the Red Sea. Why did God decide on this longer route? Well, so many times after they came out, the grumbling Israelites would have gone back into pagan Egypt! They complained about lack of food and water, about hardship and so many other things; often they would have gone back. But they could not. The Red Sea stopped them; it became a barrier to prevent them returning to the old life in Egypt. Their only way through had been by a miracle which opened the waters and, in His master plan, God used the same water to destroy their enemy. It is the same with the blood of Christ and water baptism. It is to remind every baptised believer that we cannot easily go back into the old life because when we believe and are baptised in water, this reminds us that God has made a barrier, the power of the enemy is broken, the devil has been defeated. Praise God, Satan cannot touch us, we are on the other side. Christ stands between us and Satan – water baptism is the evidence.

If you have been 'christened' or sprinkled, what about it? It will not harm you, but please be obedient to the Word of God. You should seek to be baptised in water anywhere where you can be totally immersed – in your church, a swimming pool, a river, a water tank or even as they sometimes do in Russia, in a bath in someone's home! It is a witness and demonstration of your faith. See your pastor/minister – you cannot baptise yourself. But do it now. Don't wait. Jesus is coming soon, so be ready for Him!

Part II

Prayer – Which Makes it Happen!

CHAPTER TWELVE

SPIRITUAL WARFARE

Many people talk about 'spiritual warfare'. To me this is the ability to come before the Lord in prayer, receive power, then get out there where the action is. In order to do this we need to know who we are in Christ and what authority and power we have. If we are going to respond to the enormous challenge which is facing us today we need fewer words and more action. Surely anyone who actually realises that they have power and authority and who also knows their God is going to get out and DO IT.

We need intercessors. These are generally assumed to be the ones who stay at home and pray, and we need more and more of these who are like Aaron and Hur, who held up the arms of Moses while the Israelites were in battle (Exodus 17:12). But what I also read in Scripture is that intercessors like Moses and Elijah were renowned for their action. They had the ability to confront the enemy where he was. Whether you are called to be at home or on the front line, get into action – this is all-out war. God has called us to advance, and stop retreating. With spiritual warfare the best form of defence is to ATTACK the devil in

Jesus' Name. The Bible says, 'For this cause was the Son of God manifest, to destroy the works of the devil!' (1 John 3:8). The Bible also says that we are called to do the works of Christ.

Europe is now into the greatest battle of all time. The reason why in these last days the Antichrist will be revealed – and we have all the prophecies regarding the 'Mark of the Beast', the tribulation and the other terrible destructions predicted in Revelation – is clear. The devil wants to (a) prevent the return of Christ, (b) use the 'scorched earth' policy to destroy the earth before His return, or make it a place of such destruction that Christ will not be able to rule, (c) establish his rule on earth first, controlling men and women – and this is what is happening now! The choice is between what the devil is offering and what the Bible shows God will give. We need to stop the devil by spiritual warfare. How?

1. We need authority

We have a tremendous authority here on earth, which comes from Christ through His Word: in two places we can find evidence. First, Jesus called twelve disciples in Luke 9 and then 70 in Luke 10. His command to them was simple: 'Boys, no one knows who I am, so before I come, go into all the towns and villages and in My Name preach the Gospel and heal the sick – so that when I come, they will know who I am.' Notice that here, in the command to the evangelists, He does not say 'PRAY' for the sick, simply 'HEAL THEM'! This requires AUTHORITY, and is confirmed by the report these evangelists gave when they returned. They reported that 'even the demons are

SUBJECT to us'! Why? Because they had the authority and used it.

If we believe the evidences and signs in the Bible, the literal return of Christ is very close. I personally believe that we are much further through prophecy than we realise – it is not all to be relegated to the future. So the command of Christ is relevant to today. He is repeating the urgency: 'They don't know who I am, so in My Name, preach the Gospel, heal the sick, so that when I come they will know who I am.'

The second evidence of our authority in Christ is in Mark 16 when Jesus, after His resurrection, commands His disciples to 'Go into all the world and preach the Gospel . . . ' adding, 'These signs will follow those who believe. They will lay hands on the sick and they WILL be healed.' Finally Mark says that they went forth and preached everywhere, the Lord working with them, confirming His word with SIGNS following. THIS was the demonstration and proof God used to confirm the Gospel and establish the church. I do not believe that God has changed. If we go in His Name, believing, He will confirm His word again today with SIGNS and WONDERS.

In Matthew 8, a centurion beseeched Jesus for his servant lying at home, sick of the palsy. He simply said, 'I ALSO am a man under authority' – thus recognising Christ's authority – 'just speak the word!' Once we accept the authority given us we can also become 'men under authority'.

Further confirmation of our authority comes in the promise of Jesus: 'These things shall you do and greater, because I go to My Father' (John 14:12); and Acts 1:8, 'You shall receive power after the Holy Ghost is come upon you!' Our power with God is through the baptism of the Holy Spirit, and through our relationship with God in prayer following that experience.

2. We need faith

In Matthew 17, when Jesus – with Peter, James and John – came down from the Mount of Transfiguration, He found the other disciples at the bottom, unable to heal the boy possessed by an evil spirit. Jesus said two things: first, that this kind only comes out by prayer and fasting; then secondly He rebuked His disciples' lack of faith, saying that if they had faith even as small as a grain of mustard seed they could command this mountain to move. We all accept the need of faith in our lives, especially as without it we cannot be saved, but this kind of faith is different. It is a real gift (see the gifts of the Spirit in 1 Corinthians 12), but also it is demonstrably necessary to those who are called into service. It must be a vital part of our experience if we are to engage in spiritual warfare. The believer who has not yet moved a 'mountain' has not yet begun the real task of the ministry because Jesus went on to say that 'nothing is impossible'. I challenge you to begin to act in the power and authority of your faith. So many times I have had to face the impossible and seen God move in power, and I challenge you to begin to do it yourself.

I am reminded of an experience I had while in the prison in Czechoslovakia in 1972–3 for Bible smuggling. I was forbidden to have a Bible in the prison (it was only after nine months that I managed to smuggle one in), but they gave me twelve books to read in English. This included 600 pages of the history of the communist revolution in

China. However, to my amazement, I found that one of the books was the story of Marco Polo, who was born in Venice in the thirteenth century. Together with his father and uncle, he spent most of his life-time as a merchant adventurer in China. He became a favourite of the Emperor Kublai Khan. Travelling through China with him, they came to a village where they found a group of believers. The Emperor was going to have them put to death immediately, but then he said, 'Your Bible says that if you have faith as small as a mustard seed, you can command a mountain to move and it will move! I will prove that your God is dead and that the Bible is a lie. Outside this village is a mountain. I will come back in three days, and if it has not moved, I will put you to death.' The first day the believers pleaded with God to move the mountain, but mountains don't move! The second day they chose a believer more 'holy' than themselves to plead with God. Still nothing happened. The third day, Kublai Khan returned, 'Before I kill you, I will give you one more chance. I want to see you pray,' he said. This time the desperate believers COMMANDED the mountain in Jesus' Name – AND IT MOVED! This is an historical fact recorded by Marco Polo, and because of this miracle Kublai Khan became a believer and sent Marco Polo back to Venice to bring missionaries to evangelise China!

3. We need God's vision

In Proverbs 29:18 we read, 'Where there is no vision, the people perish.' We need a strong vision, or the churches, the believers, Russia – and the rest of the world – will perish.

When Moses sent out twelve spies to view the Promised Land they all saw the same thing: a land flowing with milk and honey, with corn and grapes. They also all saw the walled cities and the giants. The difference was in the reaction. For ten, their fear of the giants and walled cities dimmed their vision. We cannot do it, it is impossible, we will be overcome. Only two, seeing the same thing, recognised the power and authority of God so that their vision of God's power blotted out their fear. In His Name and by His power nothing is impossible; we shall overcome. It is just the same today. If we really knew our God and had a vision of Him, we would attempt the impossible and take the land! It is only this kind of vision which obeys in faith that will win the unbelieving nations and people today.

4. We need obedience

The Bible says that 'by faith, Abraham obeyed and went, not knowing where he was going' (Hebrews 11:8). When I was praying over the 1995 programme in Siberia, God spoke strongly to me from 1 Chronicles 28:20 where David says to his son Solomon, 'Be strong and of good courage, and DO IT. Fear not, be not dismayed; for the LORD God, even my God is with you. He will not fail you or forsake you, until all the work is finished.'

Too often Christians wait for three things before acting: (i) till they are perfect, (ii) till they know where they're going, (iii) till they can fit it into all their other commitments. Therefore Christians rarely move. I am praying that God will send men and women with the following: (a) a burning vision, (b) a real faith, and (c) a willingness to obey Him.

Abraham was a man 'with a past' (Joshua 24:2). He was not made perfect and ready for service by extensive counselling. Instead he believed God and God accounted it as righteousness (Romans 4:3). Because of his faith in Him, God overlooked all of his sin. Where do we see the demonstration of his faith? In Hebrews 11:8 – 'by faith, Abraham obeyed'.

Do we really believe that Christ will return soon?

All the evidence is that the Lord is coming back very soon. If you believe this as I do, it will affect the way you live and what you do with your time and money. If you look at the situation in the world and the evidence of Christ's return, then what is your response?

We've got a battle on every front. The devil is facing a thousand years in chains and eternity in hell. I have seen the horror in the demons when confronted with the fires of hell. When casting one demon out in Siberia I became angry and rebuked it, saying that if it did not obey the authority of Christ I would cast it into hell fire. It answered in English, 'Not that – anything but that!' We are now entering the last great battle between the forces of Christ and the devil. The powers of the heavenlies will fight it out here on earth (Revelation 12:12). It will be the biggest conflict ever seen on earth. So great that Christ has to return, to save His people and deliver them by the power of His coming.

The devil is at war against the saints – BUT WE HAVE THE VICTORY IN JESUS' NAME!

CHAPTER THIRTEEN

GET A VISION AND MAKE IT HAPPEN!

Jesus gave us the parable of the Ten Virgins. Unfortunately, while five were prepared for the coming of the bridegroom and went into the wedding feast, five were caught unprepared because of the long wait and their lack of oil, so were excluded (Matthew 25). Surely the virgins must be symbolic of the church. Does this mean that half of the church is asleep, powerless and unprepared for the return of Christ?

We need to know God's power in us

When we see what is happening in the world today, the fulfilment of so many prophecies, and how close we are to the return of Christ, we need to act fast. Remember the great commission of Christ: 'Go into all the world and preach the Gospel!' (Mark 16:15). Remember also that the Bible says, 'For this purpose was the Son of man revealed, to destroy the works of the evil one' (1 John 3:8). In order to do these things and to see the fulfilment of all that GOD, rather than the devil, wants to do in these last days, we need to experience and know God's dynamic power in us.

In Acts 1:8 Jesus said, 'You shall receive power after the Holy Ghost is come upon you, and you shall be witnesses.' The clear promise is that HIS power would be in US. Also that we would become witnesses. A witness is one who sees something and reports on it. We need to see, experience and witness God's miraculous power in action! Not merely by sitting and waiting, but by making it happen through the power of God. Get a vision and make it happen!

In these last days, we in the church need to be filled, not just with ordinary power such as every born-again Christian receives, but with a mighty experience which the Scripture refers to as being 'baptised into' the Holy Spirit. This is an enduement with power which will enable us to speak with new tongues and work healings and miracles. I am convinced that God's Spirit in us can produce not only miraculous healings but miracles of the supernatural, such as we have experienced in Siberia. In these last awesome days nothing less than this will do. Only the fulfilment of EVERYTHING which Christ promised will become in us a mighty instrument of warfare which will win souls and demonstrate the power and glory of God to unbelieving men and nations.

One of the gifts of the Spirit referred to in 1 Corinthians 12 is the gift of faith. This is a supernatural power to believe God for the utterly impossible things. But it requires obedience and demonstration. In James 2:18 we read, 'Show me your faith . . . and I will show you my faith by my works!' In the Old Testament, Abraham's faith was such that he obeyed the call of God to leave the luxury of his life in Ur and go out and live in a tent in the wilderness, 'not knowing where he was going' (Hebrews 11:8).

We need to know our power with God

As believers we need to know the secret of our power with God. As we learn to become intercessors we begin to understand that we can have this power. There is a lot of misunderstanding about intercession. This is no formula. Rather an intercessor is one who stands before God on behalf of an individual or a nation and takes the responsibility of 'making it happen'.

Elijah made it happen

Since receiving the vision for Russia, the Lord has been speaking to me again about the fire on Carmel. In 1 Kings 18:36–37, Elijah asks God to 'let it be known . . . that Thou art God in Israel . . . that I have done all these things at Thy word . . . and that Thou hast turned their hearts back'. This marks Elijah as an intercessor who had remarkable power with God. So much so that literal fire fell from heaven and consumed the sacrifice. Not only this, but by his dynamic faith and personal relationship with God, he brought about the conversion of a WHOLE nation in a day! Literally he 'made it happen'.

If we can experience this relationship and power with God today, then we also can turn the hearts of a nation and bring fire from God – not merely evangelism, but the ability to work great miracles of divine intervention before the people, TO CONFIRM WHO GOD REALLY IS.

Moses made it happen

In Numbers 14 we see Moses' power with God. Probably one of the greatest dialogues ever recorded between man and God is this one commencing with verse 11, where God speaks very directly to Moses, complaining of the lack of response and the disobedience of Israel. Their lack of faith prompts God to say, 'How long will they not believe Me, despite all the signs which I have worked amongst them?' As a result, He threatens to destroy the whole nation. But in verse 13, in one of the most amazing scenes in Scripture, Moses dares to argue with God. He says, 'If you do so, then the Egyptians will hear and tell the other nations, all of whom have heard and seen the miraculous deliverance and mighty signs which You have worked in their midst. They will not blame Israel for their lack of faith and disobedience, but will blame You, saying that You did not have the power to deliver them.' Then Moses demonstrates the power he has with God as intercessor, saying, 'Pardon the iniquity of this people!'

God answers, 'I have pardoned, according to YOUR word' (verse 20). Moses 'made it happen'! Do you see what the intercessor has done? Moses as the intercessor has challenged God so that instead of turning His back on His people because of their weakness, because of their sin, because of their failure to evangelise and their failure to win the world, God says, 'Because of the intercessor I will renew My covenant, I will renew My power, I will renew My glory. I will send the power of My Spirit on them, backslidden as they are, fallible as they are – because you have stood before Me!'

Then God says in verse 21, in confirmation of the

further power of the intercessor (especially when compared with Elijah, who called down God's fire in 1 Kings 18), 'All the earth shall be filled with the GLORY of the Lord!' This glory is the FIRE which surrounds God, and it will fill ALL the earth.

We can make it happen!

Do you see the glory of God? Do you see that WE can have power with God, even as fallible men here on earth? In James 5:16–17 we read, 'The effectual fervent prayer of the righteous man availeth much. Elijah was a man of like passions as we are, and he prayed earnestly . . .!'

A new concept of prophetic vision

One of the most prophetic passages in the whole of the Old Testament is Deuteronomy 4:29 onwards. The first part is conditional, 'IF you will seek the Lord . . . with all your heart and with all your soul . . . ' then verse 30 is a reference to the timing – 'in the latter days'. Then we come to the prophecy in verse 32, 'Ask of the days that are past since the day of creation until now, ask from one side of Heaven to the other . . . ' We are challenged to ask a question from the whole record of history, from the east to the west, from one side of Heaven to the other, worldwide . . .

What is this prophetic question we should ask? Verse 34 gives the answer: 'Has any god ever before attempted to take a nation from within a nation by miracles, wonders and signs?' This actually related to Israel, but God spoke to me, that by faith and by the power of the intercessor, He will do this thing in Russia, beginning in Siberia, TODAY!

There is going to be a greater outpouring of God's Spirit in Russia than anywhere else in the whole world – if we will act now before the Antichrist arises. Europe (Daniel 2:41–44) is the final spiritual battleground before the attack on Israel (Ezekiel 38–39; Zechariah 12–14). Before the Lord comes, it is our task to lift up the Name of Jesus and demonstrate who He is by signs and wonders. God is saying to the church in these last days, 'I am prepared and am about to do something greater, bigger than anything that has ever been seen in the expanse of the earth, in the history of the church, and I'm about to do it NOW!'

I have seen the extent of the revival which God will bring, the signs and wonders, the miracles, the power and glory of God! Normally, in graphic terms, a prophet stands on Sunday, looks forward and prophesies what will happen on Monday. In my vision I saw the whole prophecy about Siberia and Russia so clearly, it was as if I was standing on Tuesday, not looking forward, but back on Monday and seeing it, not as a prophecy, but as an accomplished fact!

The vision is for now

When I was speaking in a church in Germany a few days before the Karlsruhe East-West Conference in 1992, a young man read a simple verse which transformed my thinking and my message for the whole conference. It was from Ezekiel 12. Immediately the Holy Spirit began to speak to me and showed me verse 21, where God spoke to Israel, saying, 'What is that proverb that you have . . . saying, the days are long and every vision fails?' Then in verse 23, God rebukes them, 'I will make this proverb cease . . . say unto them, THE DAYS ARE AT HAND AND

THE FULFILMENT OF EVERY VISION.'

Again in verse 27 the people say (concerning the prophetic vision), 'The vision he sees is for many days to come, and he prophesies of the times that are far off.' God answers them in verse 28, 'Say unto them, none of My words shall be delayed any more!'

Dramatically God was telling me that the time is NOW, the prophetic vision will be fulfilled NOW! This applies to the vision of the revival in Russia. We are in the last days and the return of Christ is NOW.

CHAPTER FOURTEEN

FAITH IS NOT FAITH UNLESS TESTED

We cannot live from meeting to meeting, just talking and singing about the power of God. We've got to 'make it happen'! God wants us to be men and women of ACTION; not passive, but people He can work through. There are three practical ways in which you can make the things of God happen in your life so that you can fulfil His call, see His miracles and become what God wants you to be. You need a faith that has been tested, a greater power in prayer and a simple obedience.

Real faith

I'm not talking about dreams, but about a vision with faith that ENABLES YOU TO DO THE JOB! It didn't take the children of Israel 40 years to travel from Egypt to Canaan. It only took 40 days! When they got to the edge of the Promised Land (Numbers 13) Moses sent out twelve spies. They all SAW exactly the same thing – a beautiful land with mountains and rivers. It was everything God had promised – plenty of wheat and corn, grapes so big they could hardly carry them! They all also saw the problems: the giants, the cities with walls and many soldiers, every city with an army to defend it. When they got back to Moses ten of the men said, 'It's wonderful, much better than Egypt. It's exactly what God promised – but it's impossible! How can we go in? We'll be defeated! We don't have enough people, we're not strong enough . . . ' But two of the spies said, 'Yes, we saw the same land flowing with milk and honey – we saw the same walled cities with their armies and the giants – but with God, nothing is impossible! Our God works miracles . . . God will destroy the enemy. God will give us everything He promised. All we have to do is take it!'

All twelve spies saw the same land of prosperity and promise, but only two had the faith to go in and take possession! They knew that nothing was impossible with God. But because Israel listened to the ten who were in the majority, because they did not have enough faith to act, they had to wait 40 years in the wilderness to achieve the same thing.

We all see the promises of God – we have the same Bible. God's promises are rich, and they are for us. You and I are standing on the edge of a promised land. It is everything that we want and God wants us to have – NOW! The danger is that we are not looking at the promise but at the problems. We look at other people who have faith to believe, but for us we think it's impossible. Yes, we know the promises, but we don't do it because we see too many giants in the way.

Yes, you will eventually enter into God's promises – finance, healing, ministry – but why wait the 40 years as Israel did? God is challenging us to test our faith – to do it now. He's calling us to a land of power, of miracles, of signs and wonders, and He wants us to go in and possess it. Don't wander in the desert. Go in faith and take what God has promised! This is His challenge: take the land, don't look at the problems, LOOK AT GOD'S POWER. If He said it, He'll do it – God cannot lie!

Our faith is not faith at all until it is put to the test. Without testing, without proving it, it's just something in the mind. Peter wrote, ' . . . so that the TESTING OF YOUR FAITH, being more precious than gold that perishes, though it be tried with fire, might be found unto praise and honour and glory at the appearing of Jesus Christ!' (1 Peter 1:6–7).

God puts this test of faith in all our lives. He tested my faith. When I had cancer in my throat many years ago, I said to the Lord, 'If You want me to go to Russia, I want a miracle.' God worked that miracle and I had to leave my home, my security, and go to Russia!

When I was in prison for smuggling Bibles into Russia I was sentenced to what could have been ten years. I was not allowed a Bible, but I reminded the Lord that in Acts 16, when Paul and Silas were imprisoned, they began to praise the Lord, and He sent an earthquake and freed them. By faith I asked the Lord to do the same for me. He answered, and opened my prison doors by a miracle!

Real prayer

James 5:16 says, 'The effectual fervent prayer of a righteous man avails much.' Powerful prayer works! The original Greek of the Bible often uses a special word for power: dunamis. It signifies miraculous, wonder-working power. From it we get the words 'dynamo' (which generates power) and 'dynamite' (the explosive). If you want prayer to work, to change your circumstances, then it must generate power. And it has to be like dynamite. If you put an ordinary explosive against a wall, its energy disperses into space. But dynamite does not dissipate its energy – it pushes the wall down! That's what our prayer must be like. It's got to move mountains! We must learn how to talk to God until our praying will move every mountain, every obstruction, everything that stands between us and the fulfilment of God's promises.

Real obedience

Hebrews 11:8 says, 'Abraham, when he was called to go out . . . obeyed; and he went out, not knowing whither he went.' Abraham lived as a wealthy cattle rancher in Ur of the Chaldees. He had everything – farm, cattle, money, position. But God called him to leave everything and go. And he went out, never receiving the end of the promise, living as a nomad in a tent, but in obedience. Even when called to offer his only son Isaac as a sacrifice, he obeyed.

The secret of power with God is in obedience. It is the final part of the three-fold way to 'make it happen'. On my first visit to Siberia many years ago I was asked to explain to a group of pastors how I hear from God. I thought for a moment, then it was as if the Holy Spirit reminded me. Often when I am at home I like to read at the breakfast table. My wife tries to get my attention and keeps talking to me, but I am so busy reading that I do not hear. I take no notice.

Often we are like that with God. He is always talking to us, but we are too busy to listen, so we don't do what He says. Eventually God stops speaking. If we do not obey Him, He stops asking us.

To me the greatest miracle in the Bible is the first, when Jesus turned water into wine at the wedding in Cana. Mary, His mother, had never seen Him work a miracle (this was before any of the many miracles which were to follow), yet she went to the servants at the wedding and said to them, 'In a few minutes Jesus will ask you to do something incredibly stupid [to put water into wine jars]. Don't ask any questions, just do it!' The real miracle wasn't turning water into wine; it was Mary saying, 'Just do it!' In other words, if you want to see miracles, just do it. It's about obedience!

In 1988 God told me to bring people from all over Eastern Europe (still under communism) into a conference in West Germany. People said, 'There's an Iron Curtain. They cannot come from the East. You have no money. It's impossible!' But God told me to do it, so I obeyed, and God worked miracles! Four thousand came – 600 of them made the impossible journey from all over the East. And God paid all the bills! If God says 'Do it!' then do it!

God told me to go to Bulgaria in 1990. When I said we should take a stadium, my friends laughed at me: 'It's impossible. This is a communist country. We don't have the money. We won't get permission from the government.' But we went to the directors of the stadium. They laughed too: 'You cannot rent the stadium for evangelism! It belongs to the communist party. We don't believe in God!' I prayed, 'Oh God, I need a miracle.' Suddenly they relented: 'You cannot rent the stadium, but there is nothing to stop us giving it to you free!' The revival began from that day and spread through the whole of Bulgaria. Why?

They had said it was impossible, but God said, 'Do it!'

In 1994 God told me, 'Go and evangelise the whole of Siberia!' Siberia is 52 times the size of Great Britain and four times that of North America! We would need 400 team members and 100 tonnes of equipment for 17 crusades, each crusade 17 days (I had to preach in every crusade). We were to be there for three months – the total cost £1 million. We had no money and people laughed at me, 'It's impossible!' But God told me to go. We went, and God gave us the money and He worked the miracles! But too often we fail to go in and possess the land. Faith is only faith when it's tested. When God says 'Do it!' you must obey Him.

Faith, prayer, obedience

If we want to possess God's promises in our lives, we must be practical. It takes faith to put the vision into action, prayer to move the mountains and obedience to receive the Holy Spirit's power that will enable us to do the job. Leave the questions to Him to solve and do what He says! The Bible says, 'To obey is better than sacrifice' (1 Samuel 15:22).

CHAPTER FIFTEEN

THE REGION BEYOND

We need to have a spiritual awakening. We need a new power from God – the power of the Holy Spirit in us today, as on the Day of Pentecost – but the key which will release that power into our lives now is a new level of faith in Jesus Christ.

In Matthew 17, when Jesus' disciples failed to cast out the demon from the epileptic boy and then asked him why, He rebuked them for their unbelief: 'If you have faith as a grain of mustard seed, you shall say to this mountain, remove hence to yonder place and it shall remove,' AND AFTER IT DOES, 'nothing will be impossible to you!' (Matthew 17:20). What a challenge! While I was preaching this, God showed me the hidden key.

Unbelief brings failure . . .

Jesus rebuked His disciples because they did not have the faith to do what they had to do – they had been given a specific job and when they were left to do it, they failed! Jesus spoke to them very strongly. Because they knew that they had failed publicly and He had rebuked them openly, they came to Him privately to ask what had gone wrong, in those immortal words, 'Why?' 'Why could we not cast out this spirit and heal the boy?'

. . . faith is the KEY

There is something hidden here. Yes, Jesus said in answer to their question, 'If you had faith . . . you could move mountains.' But the real secret of power is hidden. We get stuck at the thought that mortal man could move anything bigger than himself. We agonise over the reality of moving that mountain. We call our friends to stand with us in believing prayer because this mountain is proving harder than we thought to move. Then when it happens – that miracle, that healing or financial solution – we become so excited (as I experienced so many times personally) that we drop the real key down the drain in our excitement!

The disciples had missed the opportunity of releasing the greatest power into their lives. Jesus was putting a key in their hands, and if they would only use this key, their lives would never be the same again! For me, searching and hungry for more of God's power in my life, I saw what I had been waiting for: there is a spiritual 'region beyond'.

We need an awakening . . .

We need an awakening to realise that God has a power and a glory far greater than anything we have ever seen yet. Are we, in our spiritual experience, ready to cross the barrier, to move into something so big we could hardly dream about it?

I understand, scientifically, that none of us as normal

human beings ever uses the real capacity of our brain. In other words the capacity of the human brain far exceeds anything that we could imagine. Even the Einsteins of this world only use part, possibly even less than 5 per cent of the capacity of the human brain.

Let me ask you, then, how big is God's power? Who was the greatest man in the Bible – Moses, Elijah, Paul, Peter? With all the miracles they saw God perform, did any one of them ever see more than 5 per cent of God's power? How big is our God? Twenty times bigger, a thousand times bigger than what they saw? When I begin to look at how big my God really is, suddenly I want this key – the one Jesus showed His disciples – to open a door into a totally new experience. It is as if all my life I have been looking only at a darkened mirror image of God, and now . . .

. . . to the 'normal' Christian life

Of all the gifts of God, FAITH is the greatest – it's the KEY to the 'normal' Christian life. There are nine gifts, which you only receive after you have been baptised in the Holy Spirit (have you received . . . since you believed?): three VOCAL gifts – speaking in tongues, interpretation of tongues, and prophecy; three INTELLECTUAL gifts – the word of knowledge, the word of wisdom, and the discerning of spirits; and three PRACTICAL gifts (I love the practical gifts) – healing, working of miracles, and the gift of faith (1 Corinthians 12). These are the normal everyday gifts of the Holy Spirit to the believer. By the same power with which you speak in tongues, you also heal the sick and work miracles! Paul asks, 'Does everybody work miracles?' What a challenge! Does every church work miracles? But this is the NORMAL Christian life! Cry out to God that He will fill you with the Holy Ghost and power!

Faith is what you DO

Are you living a normal Christian life? Do you have the gift of faith? This is NOT an intellectual gift. Faith is nothing to do with your education or with what you think – it's what you DO. Faith is ACTION. Hebrews 11:1 describes faith as SUBSTANCE and EVIDENCE, something solid. It's not something intellectual; it's the most PRACTICAL gift God can give.

Do you want to please God?

I would say that if you want to please God, there is one thing that gives more glory to Him than anything else; one thing that will please Him more than anything else.

Even in human relationships, whether in marriage or in business or just in friendship, if that relationship is not built on a mutual trust between the partners, sooner or later it will fail. Yet that trust is probably one of the hardest things to establish and the easiest to lose. When you say that you BELIEVE God, when you have FAITH in Him (Hebrews 11:6), it means that you TRUST Him more than anybody in Heaven or on earth. This brings more glory to God than anything else, because it is the only basis of a permanent lasting relationship and means you are saying to Him, 'I know You cannot fail me, because You are God!' When you REALLY BELIEVE what He SAYS, this will change your life.

Afraid of the power of God

I have seen many miracles. In a period of five years, we recorded more than 20,000 healings in Russia and Ukraine. I have a very long record with the KGB! One year I arrived in a city in Russia and they were waiting to stop me preaching, but their biggest problem was not the preaching, it was the miracles of healing! They are not afraid of preachers. They are afraid of the power of God! They asked me, 'What is your authority to heal the sick?' We opened the Word of God and showed them Mark 16: 'This is what God tells us to do – it's in the Bible, "Lay hands on the sick and they WILL be healed!" We're going to do what the Bible says.' And they couldn't stop us!

Faith moves mountains

Thirty years ago I was put in a communist prison in Czechoslovakia. They said that if I did not give up my faith, they would not let me out alive. The only way to get out was to become a communist! They gave me books to re-educate me, and one was the true story of Marco Polo (a merchant venturer from Italy, 1254–1354) and his travels in China with the Emperor, Kublai Khan, grandson of Genghis Khan.

One day the Chinese Emperor and Marco Polo came to a village and found a small group of believers. The Emperor was very cruel and commanded his soldiers to kill them. But he said, 'Before I kill you, I will prove that your God is dead and your Bible is a lie. Your Bible says that if you've got faith like a mustard seed, you will see a mountain and command it to move, and it will go. Outside your village is a mountain – I'm going to give you three days to move it!'

So Marco Polo said that they cried out the first day, 'Oh God, we're going to die! Move the mountain!' And the mountain did not move. The second day, they found one man, a shoemaker, 'more spiritual' than the rest and they made him do the praying. He prayed all day, 'Oh God, we're going to die! Move the mountain!' And still the mountain did not move. The third day, the Emperor came back and commanded his soldiers to line the believers up outside the village and cut off their heads! But first he said, 'I gave you three days to move the mountain and it's still there! You have no God, your Bible is a lie, and I want you to die knowing that there is no God. You must pray one more time while I watch you! Then I'll kill you.'

In that communist prison, with no Bible, this is what I read: Marco Polo said that this time those believers began to pray differently. They looked at that mountain, and they began to command it to move in the Name of Jesus. As the Emperor watched, the mountain MOVED! He became a believer and sent Marco Polo back to Italy to bring missionaries to evangelise China. Because of that one miracle, the whole of China was opened to the Gospel, and today there are more than 100 million believers in China. Why? Because God moved the mountain.

Through that true story God began to speak to me: 'David, your mountain is the prison. If you have the faith to believe, I will open the prison and release you, BY A MIRACLE.' I began to call on God, to claim a miracle, and God sent the miracle! After I had been there only ten months, not ten years, exactly on the day God showed me six months earlier, God sent the British Prime Minister from London to Prague, just to release me, and I flew home with him! It was on television and reported in newspapers worldwide – the miracle that God had done!

Revolution

Jesus said to His disciples, 'You only have to have the smallest faith in the world!' This is how we begin. Coming out of the prison was not the end; it was a beginning. It was a REVOLUTION in my life! I UNDERSTOOD from that moment that with God NOTHING is impossible for the rest of my life! In that moment God had put in my hands a new key.

CHAPTER SIXTEEN

THE HOLY SPIRIT GOES TO WAR!

Today the Holy Spirit is declaring war! Isaiah 59:19 says, 'They shall fear the Name of the LORD from the West and see His glory from the rising of the sun in the East. And when the enemy shall come in, like a flood the Holy Spirit of God shall lift up a standard against him.' To lift up a standard (flag) is a military expression which means that you are going to war. In this age and generation the Holy Spirit is declaring war on the devil. The devil IS defeated. When Christ died on the cross, He broke the devil's power. Satan, hell and death ARE defeated in Jesus Christ. But the purpose of God is for the power of the Holy Spirit to come into the church to make the church a dynamic army. We've got to rise up in the church today, become more militant, more active, making evangelism the priority, because we've got to see the glory of God in the whole earth as the fulfilment of this prophecy.

The world is perishing and dying, and when I look at what the devil is now doing in the world, I want to do everything I can to speed Christ's return. I want to see more of the glory of God than has ever been seen before;

more of the power, of the love of God; more miracles, more repenting and finding a complete salvation. It's my heart's desire to be involved in the preparation for the return of the Messiah. I want to be doing something to prepare the way for Jesus when He comes back.

The whole world has got to hear about our Jesus before He comes, so don't be a bystander. There is a job everyone can do. No one is too old, too feeble, too young to pray! I have given to God everything I have – my life, my time, all my energy. You can give from what you have.

Pearl of greatest price

Jesus said that if you are a businessman trading in pearls, and you have a whole batch of small ones, and then you see somebody with that big one, bigger than any you have seen before, you'll sell everything you've got. You've got to sacrifice to get the pearl of greatest price! The secret of power with God is sacrifice. Solomon built the Temple and at the dedication (2 Chronicles 6–7) he climbed up and put himself on the altar, and kneeled on the altar. That was the only time fire fell on the Temple. Fire never fell on the Temple when they offered sacrifices of bulls and goats and sheep. The only time the fire of God fell on the Temple was when a man put himself on the altar. If you want the fire in your life, you've got to put yourself on the altar.

There is a battle for the survival of the truth WITHIN the church. Much of the truth is being watered down and lost. We've got to get back to the fire and the power of an old-fashioned Gospel, the Gospel of the blood of Jesus and the fire of the Holy Ghost! The evidence of the Holy Ghost is His power in YOU. We need more evidence! We need breakthrough faith!

O God, put a hunger in my heart for righteousness, holiness; for the real fire and the real anointing of the Holy Spirit. O God, make me so hungry that I don't count the cost; that I will hunger and thirst after You. Only You can satisfy, O God. Only Your power, only Your fire can give the answer that I need – nothing else. I want to see Your glory, not just in Heaven, but on earth. Do something new in my heart today!

What is in your heart? Search your heart. What is the thing that is most important? You can try to give an answer, but God knows the real thing that is uppermost in your heart. If He said He would give you the thing that is most important in your heart, in your life, right now, do you really know what God would give you? He WILL give it you, but you must WANT it more than anything, and you are going to have to sacrifice to get it. You are going to have to sell the little pearls to get the big one. But in a deal like this, you don't buy first, you sell first! You can't buy until you've sold. Are you willing to let go of the little pearls? They may be precious, they may be wonderful, but there may be something you have to get rid of in order to get the reality, what you really want. Don't let go of God until you get it!

Part III
The Reality of Faith

CHAPTER SEVENTEEN

FAITH IS A CHALLENGE TO OUR ABILITY TO BELIEVE

An interesting 'window' on faith is found in Numbers 13. Moses and the whole of Israel had halted on the borders of the Promised Land after their arduous journey, which had lasted 40 days. There they were, within sight of their goal, the fulfilment of all God's promises within their grasp. Surely this was all that they could ask for, the ultimate reward for the sufferings they had endured, both in the last days in Egypt and in the travelling. This was the reason why God had performed all the outstanding miracles, both in Egypt and in the crossing of the Red Sea, in order to give them deliverance and to fulfil His promise to give them this land.

But still one thing had to happen before they could appropriate all the blessings of God which had been so clearly promised and prophesied. This was their 'Iron Curtain', the final barrier. One final step and all that they had longed and prayed for would be theirs. One step and the veil that covered their eyes would be lifted and they would see one of the most beautiful and dramatic things that man has ever seen (and few are allowed to actually see this): the REASON why God works great and powerful miracles. His purpose NOW revealed! After all, Abraham only acted in faith: He never saw the fulfilment.

But this one final step was not taken! It was to demand a faith beyond their ability. How often are believers today within sight of everything that they are desiring – often with earnest prayer and with the clear knowledge that God HAS promised . . . yet that final step is not taken? They don't go in and possess the land. It occurs in the realms of healing, finance, evangelism and missions, possibly even revival – certainly in most areas of our lives and especially our service for God.

What was the one thing that hindered them?

Moses sent out twelve spies to view the land WHICH GOD HAD PROMISED TO GIVE. These all saw the same things: a land flowing with milk and honey. Green, green grass, corn better than Egypt, fruit so big it had been just a dream when they were captives, rivers and lakes of freshest sweet water, plenty of fish (Galilee is famous – I've eaten its fish, so I know), lovely valleys for the cattle, beautiful mountains (one snow-capped all year round) – literally springs in the valleys and streams in the desert. Far better than the Egypt they had left. It was everything that God had promised and more! Of course they saw the walled cities, soldiers guarding them and the fact that some of the inhabitants were giants. This was not Eden, not an empty land – they would have to fight for their inheritance!

The important fact was that all twelve saw precisely the same things, stood in the same places, had the same God. But when they returned to Moses, their reports differed in certain essentials. All twelve told the Israelites, that yes this was THE Promised Land, no disagreement, but the majority (ten against two) said that it was impossible to enter. After they had all excitedly shared the joy that the fulfilment would bring, and yes it was all that God had said and more, the ten said that the difficulties were too great. There was no way that they could defeat the enemies and actually possess the promise! They were looking in human terms, seeing only their own limited resources and accepting failure as the norm. Only two said that they agreed with everything the ten had said, but because God WAS with them, they could possess the promise now. He would not fail them. They reminded the whole of Israel of all that God had done in the past, how He was still with them and that in His Name they would win, however hard the fight!

It was God's decision to abide by the majority decision, which compelled the whole nation of Israel to wander in a barren wilderness for 40 more years before they finally entered the Promised Land. What was the one thing that went wrong? They had a lack of the RIGHT kind of faith.

Step into faith

Two of the spies, Joshua and Caleb, knew their God and had an implicit faith in Him. They knew that God cannot fail, that what He says He does. They were willing to take that vital step over into the promises BY ACTING IN FAITH.

We need this kind of faith that does see both sides, that does see every problem, but still believes God. Sometimes in my own walk with God in faith, I am faced with these same questions. I am convinced that I see even more of the problems than those who don't have the faith! This makes this kind of faith an even greater miracle. This illustration from Israel raises two questions: was the fulfilment of God's promise worth fighting for; and could they have had the faith?

Believer, YOU are so near to the fulfilment in your own life! Why look at the problems which make the fulfilment impossible? Look at Him and then go in and claim the land!

You want that kind of faith

Then look at this scripture in 1 Corinthians 12 about the nine gifts of the Holy Spirit. Have you received the Holy Spirit? Do you speak with tongues as the disciples did on the day of Pentecost (Acts 2)? When we talk about faith, Jesus said in Mark 16:18, 'These signs will follow those who believe . . . they will speak with new tongues.' Today this powerful and demonstrative gift is experienced not just by the Pentecostals, but, as a result of the charismatic renewal, throughout most sections of the body of Christ. I believe that it is part of the ministry within the church worldwide and a fulfilment of the prophecies of Joel 2 and Acts 2: 'I will pour out My Spirit on all flesh and they shall prophesy.'

But this gift of tongues which is blessing the church throughout the world in these last days is only one of nine gifts. For in 1 Corinthians 12:9–11 Paul says that the same Spirit also gives faith, gifts of healing and the working of miracles. So faith along with healing and the working of miracles is an operation of the same Spirit, and we can ask and receive these gifts! In another way, you cannot speak with tongues by your own power, only through the Holy Spirit. And by the same Holy Spirit you can heal the sick, work miracles and have the gift of faith!

However, if this is a GIFT of the Holy Spirit, it must be different from any human gift. Just as the gift of tongues is a supernatural power to speak in an 'unknown tongue', so the gift of faith is SUPERNATURAL. We all have faith on a simple level. The Bible says that we are saved by faith, so every believer has faith. But this GIFT OF FAITH is something far greater, an operation of a SUPER power in our lives by the Spirit. This is what set the two spies, Joshua and Caleb, apart from the other ten. This is what sets men and women apart today. To me it is the greatest of the nine gifts and the one which I ask the Holy Spirit to give me more of than any other gift, because it is the key to the operation of all the others.

Just do it!

To me the most outstanding miracle of all those Jesus performed was the first one He did at the wedding feast in Cana of Galilee. It took a woman to make it happen – one simple demonstration of faith in action. We need to thank God for women of faith!

Mary, His mother, had never seen her son perform a single miracle in the 30 years since His birth. Yet when she saw the problem at the wedding reception that the wine had run out, she went to the staff and told them that her son would shortly ask them to do something incredibly stupid. He would tell them to put water into the empty wine jars! All she said was, 'However stupid it may sound, whatever He says, YOU do it!' That's all it took for Jesus to perform His first miracle. One woman, and a strong prophetic word: 'Whatever He says, however stupid it might appear, don't argue . . . DO IT!' That is one of the great secrets of FAITH . . . do it! Don't ask questions, don't doubt. It's going to be a miracle anyway!

That's what the ten spies needed – to just do it. That's what God is saying to you right now as you read this. Faith is action . . . do it! Faith is never passive, always active. Men of faith are always men of action and in the eyes of the world they often appear stupid, their actions defy logic. But the interesting thing is that God honours these men above others – they please Him! Without faith it is impossible to please God (Hebrews 11:6). I have always said that I want to live a life of seeing miracles. I want *Eurovision*, my ministry, to be a ministry built on the miraculous. I know that this means living on the edge, living in excitement and anticipation every day. 'Please, my Father, I want to have real faith. Holy Spirit, I ask you, give me this kind of faith in my life, now!'

Obedience

One last word on faith is found in the experience of Abraham. The record of Hebrews 11:8 is that, in obedience to the command of God, Abraham left the comparative riches of his life in Ur of the Chaldees to begin a nomadic life in tents. Coming as he did from a very modern civilisation with a prosperous lifestyle, where he owned property and vast herds of cattle, his implicit obedience to the call and command of God to leave it all is the reason for this testimony in the great 'Faith Chapter'. Such obedience that enabled him to go without question – 'not knowing where he was going', as the Scripture says – was a remarkable evidence of his faith. This means that a condition, or at least a demonstration, of faith is a willingness to obey.

CHAPTER EIGHTEEN

MIRACLES DON'T COME EASY

A believer who had been praying a long time without result for a sick, believing relative raised this question in one of my meetings: 'Sometimes I'm strong, but sometimes I doubt, even though I don't want to, and I'm afraid I'm losing my faith for this healing. I believe, but in practice it's hard. How can one deal with this?'

I have to admit that in my own ministry I have to face similar problems, not necessarily in healing, but in some other area where I need more faith. Every New Year I like to take a few days away from the ministry, to be alone with the Lord and to spend time in serious prayer. In one of these times I was praying over this very issue – how to receive a stronger gift of faith, how to receive something by faith which is absolutely impossible to the human mind.

I believe that there is a big difference between healing for the believer in the church and healing for unbelievers. As an evangelist, with the unbeliever, you get one shot – often they are there only one time, not only to hear the Gospel, but to hear about Christ Himself for the first time – therefore they need to see and experience something in order to bring them to faith. They are not in the church, and if they don't experience something through the Holy Spirit which will miraculously make Christ a reality in their lives, they are not going to be in the church! So it's important that our contact with that person is 'complete'. But if you are dealing with people who are already in the church, sometimes it is a question of BUILDING their faith. I know from the Bible that nothing is impossible, but in order to receive, there must be a building process, a growing in faith, not giving up. This is when you must fast and pray and believe that God WILL do it! To receive that kind of faith which will work a miracle in your own life, you must be totally convinced: (a) that nothing is impossible with your God; (b) that He wants to work that miracle in you; (c) that you know when!

I was healed from throat cancer 40 years ago, but I was sick for three months before I came to the spiritual, with God where the miracle happened – three months in spiritual growth, followed by a sudden revelation, an explosion – and in that moment the healing was instantaneous! When I was in a communist prison 30 years ago for Bible smuggling, I was almost one year in the prison, believing that God would work the miracle to get me out, but that year was the best year of my life! Yes, I was separated from my wife and children – my youngest daughter was only three years old – but I grew all the time in my experience with God. It was a testing of my faith, but when God did it, it was sudden, a big miracle! I travelled the world for two years afterwards, talking about that miracle. I preached to more than a million people, sometimes 10,000 at a time, and a quarter of a million came to Christ because of that testimony! But the miracle took one year of prayer. I'm a coward and from the first day I cried, 'Oh God, get me out!' In the early days I thought that they would torture me, then simply throw me out of the country, but God didn't get me out!

However, if He had answered my first prayers and released me from the prison within one or two days, what would have happened? Suppose God had organised things 'extremely well' and got me out of prison really quickly. I would not be evangelising in Russia the way I do now. I would not have the ministry I have today. The longer I stayed in the prison, the bigger the miracle became. In the end it was the British Prime Minister, Harold Wilson, who came to Czechoslovakia, just to get me out! I was not thrown out of the 'back door'! I was released in a blaze of publicity! That's God! But the whole miracle took one year to prepare. I didn't let go of God, even in the darkest days of despair, I knew, I believed, but it hurt and it was hard. If only you could know how bad those days I spent in prison were!

It's the same with you. Hold on. Don't let go of God! God WILL do it! If it takes three months, three years, God WILL do it.

And if you doubt, don't feel that God will abandon you because of this. Let me encourage you. About three weeks before I was released from the prison (and God had told me the exact day I would get out of the prison), all the pressure in there got so much, I had a heart attack. They took me to the prison hospital and gave me an ECG. They had no medicine, so they just sent me back to my cell, and I cried out, 'Oh God, why have I had a heart attack? I'm not believing! If I really believed that I was coming out in three weeks, I wouldn't be having a heart attack, I'd be dancing for joy! Oh God, I've let go of my faith! Oh God, forgive me!' And God did! Three weeks later, I came out!

God understands. We're human! Only God is divine! We're going to fail sometimes. Even I fail God. I'm not a 'holy man' – but I do trust God, and I love God. God looks on your heart. Look at the times when Peter failed Jesus. Isn't that true?

If you are believing for healing, for yourself or others, healing is part of the atonement of Christ. Matthew 8:16–17 says that Jesus healed all who were sick in order that the words of the prophet Isaiah would be fulfilled: 'He Himself took our infirmities and bore our sicknesses' (Isaiah 53:4).

We don't live in a perfect world, but in a sinful world. Let me ask this question: is every single believer living without any sin? Let's be truthful – we do fail God. Even Paul said, 'The good things I would do, I don't do, and the bad things I don't want to do, I do!' Yes, there is forgiveness through the blood of Christ. That is why John said to the believers, 'I write unto you that you sin not, but if any man sin we have an advocate with the Father' (1 John 2:1).

It's the same with healing. Yes, we should be without sin, but the fact is the devil is in the world and we're tempted and tested every day. It's the same with healing: we accept that colds and flu are infectious, that accidents happen to all of us. We suffer cuts and bruises, headaches, toothache and sometimes broken limbs. When our children suffer from mysterious symptoms we consult the doctor. But with healing, God CAN do it, God WANTS to do it, but healing doesn't always happen. Sometimes the devil gets in the way, sometimes it is a question of our choice, sometimes a question of even our understanding of what

God wants to do in our lives. Have you ever had a financial problem? God wants to either prevent us getting into the problem in the first place, or deliver us out of it. But does this always happen, or do we sometimes suffer?

Yes, all these things WILL be resolved, they WILL happen when Christ returns. That's the final victory, and the devil will have to sit in my old prison! Then, everything will be perfect – no more death, no more tears. Calvary was our 'D'-Day when Christ made the victory possible, but 'V'-Day (final victory) is when Christ returns to earth, and at the moment we're living in the in-between.

Miracles don't come easily. You might think I talk about miracles as though they grow on trees. They don't. When I had the cancer in my throat and when I was in prison, God said the same thing to me: 'Do you want to go the easy way or the hard way?' I'm a coward, so I said, 'Tell me the easy way!' With the cancer, God said, 'The easy way is you have the operation. You'll lose your voice,' – the cancer was on my vocal cord – 'but you can learn to speak using your stomach muscles, and you won't die. I'll be with you!' Then I said, 'If that's the easy way, tell me the hard way!' I chose the hard way, because when I said, 'What happens if I choose the hard way?' He said, 'I'll work a miracle!'

Exactly the same thing happened in the prison. I said, 'Oh God, get me out of this hell!'

'Do you want the easy way or the hard way?'

'Tell me the easy way!'

'All right, you stay in prison ten years, I'll never leave you, they won't kill you or starve you to death . . .'

'Then tell me the hard way. Tell me the difference!'

God said to me, 'The hard way will bring a powerful miracle!'

I chose the hard way, and the miracle.

Miracles DON'T come easy. While driving to a preaching engagement some of my staff were with me in the car, and we were praying. I said to God, 'I'm tired of talking about the miracle of my cancer and the miracle of my release from prison. I want a new miracle, a bigger one, NOW!' Then I realised what I had said, and my staff remember I cried out to God, 'Oh God, hold me by the hand while I go through the suffering that will bring the miracle.' Do you understand? Miracles do not come easy. When in my most recent miracle I had gone to the hospital with suspected lung cancer, one of my daughters who is a nurse and was with me at the time said, 'Dad, don't be afraid when they diagnose the cancer. Unless they prove that you have it, you will have no evidence of a miracle when God heals you!'

CHAPTER NINETEEN

HOW TO WALK ON WATER

Jesus' disciples got into a ship, but the ship was now in the middle of the sea tossed with waves because the wind was against them. In the fourth watch of the night Jesus went to them, walking on the sea, and when the disciples saw Him, they were troubled, saying, 'It's a spirit!' and they cried out in fear. But Jesus spoke to them, 'It is I. Don't be afraid!' Peter answered, 'Lord, if it's You, bid me to come to You on the water!' And He said, 'Come!' When Peter had come down out of the ship he walked on the water to go to Jesus. But when he saw the wind boisterous he was afraid and, beginning to sink, he cried out, 'Lord, save me!' (Matthew 14:22–30).

Jesus wanted to escape from the crowd, so He sent His disciples away and went up the mountain to pray until the middle of the night. Now the Sea of Galilee is not that wide, but in all that time the disciples could not get that boat across the water because of the storm that was raging. And in the middle of the storm, Jesus began to walk on the water towards the ship. I've heard people try and explain this miracle and they imagine that the sea was very still and calm, but in actual fact the wind was strong, the waves were high and Jesus was walking on top of these waves!

I've been on a ship in a storm more than once. On one occasion, I was visiting some pastors in Greece, and a friend of mine who has a yacht invited me to go sailing with him. It was November. On the second day we ran into a violent storm. My friend, who was supposed to be the captain sailing the ship, disappeared below and left me alone on deck wondering what he was going to do. I called down to him, 'The wind is too strong for the sails. The ship's going further and further over!' 'Oh, I'm not afraid,' he said. 'I've never been in a storm as strong as this, but I've never sailed with an evangelist before. You're a man of God, you pray and I'll stay down here!' I tell you, I did pray and God worked a miracle. The storm eased and we came safely into a harbour on a nearby island.

So Jesus was walking on top of the stormy sea, but notice the time! Time with God is so important. If only you and I knew the time that God has chosen, it would make so much difference to us! Here it was the fourth watch in the night. This is the most dangerous and most difficult hour in the night – the time when most people die, when the body temperature is at its lowest. It's the time when some of the biggest fears and the biggest problems come, just before the new day dawns. It is so significant that when Jesus is walking towards the disciples in that storm-tossed ship, the time that He chooses is the darkest hour, when the storm is at its highest. But Jesus is there! In your life and mine there are many times when we need the power of God to deliver us, but God's timing is perfect, coming at the darkest hour, when the storm is at its fiercest and our need is the greatest.

I have learned after more than 50 years of ministry that God always answers prayer. And I want to encourage you. God never fails – He cannot fail. But to get the answer at the right hour we have to be ready, we have to be obedient, and God will answer – at the last minute. In my life God so often answers one minute before midnight. One minute before the crisis erupts. We have many kinds of problems, many different needs, but I believe in miracles. Do you? Then let me warn you of two things!

First, God does not work miracles alone! He needs people to be involved in them. When He miraculously fed 5,000, He first needed 5,000 hungry people, as well as a boy with five loaves and two fishes. When He walked on the water, the miracle also involved the storm and the disciples. In order that your miracle can happen, God needs you to become part of the miracle.

Second, you can't have a miracle without a problem! If that boat had not been in a storm on the sea, there would have been no miracle with Jesus walking on the water. If you want to see miracles, God is going to use your problem, your difficulty, your crisis in order to work the miracle. That crisis that you have – that sickness, that cancer, that arthritis, that financial problem – God will use this to create a miracle.

Every one of us can be in a storm, just like these disciples in the boat. When the disciples saw Him walking on the water their first reaction was fear. They thought they'd seen a ghost – they didn't realise it was Jesus. They were so afraid because they were convinced their boat was going to sink and they didn't believe they would last the night. In the darkest hour of your night, when your financial problems are the greatest, when your sickness is getting worse, when you're crippled with pain, when you cannot escape from alcohol or the power of drugs, in that dark hour, there is one person who will always be there – Jesus. And He chooses the darkest, the hardest, moment to come and walk towards you in order that He can work your miracle.

But in order that this water-walking miracle could happen, Jesus came towards those disciples. In the darkest hour, when the storm was at its strongest, only one man out of all the disciples in the boat called out. Then Jesus said, 'It is I. Don't be afraid.' Peter answered, 'Is it really You? Are You really there? I need a miracle now – I cannot wait. Jesus, if it is You, call me to get out of the boat. I'll know it's You if I can walk on the water.' Peter then got out of the comparative security of that boat, in the blackest, darkest moment of the night, in the middle of the storm and actually began to walk on the waves!

I want to encourage you, whatever the crisis in your life – whether it's sin, drugs, alcohol, demon possession, a broken home, sickness or financial problems, whether you're crippled, you're blind, you're deaf – in the darkest moment in your life, in the moment of your greatest tragedy, in the moment of your greatest suffering, when you're hurting more than you've ever hurt before, Jesus is there. He's not forgotten you – He's walking nearer to you. Jesus said, 'I will be with you always.' Every day, every hour, in the middle of every storm, in the middle of every sickness, even in a hospital bed, or lying on the road as the result of a car accident, Jesus will always come. Whatever the crisis, there's never a moment when He's not there.

In the middle of that storm Peter saw Jesus and said, 'If it's You, call me to come.' I want to tell you, Jesus is calling you to get out of your sin. He's calling you to come out of your sickness. Will you say, 'Jesus, if it's You, if You're real, call me and I will come'? But how many people will leave the comparative security of their crisis to actually come onto the waves only by looking at Jesus and hearing His call?

Once in Bulgaria I was telling the people about the love and the power and the miracles of God. At the front was an old man, crippled. He could only walk with difficulty with sticks. But the power of God fell on him as he listened. Suddenly his face lit up as if he knew that Jesus was there. He jumped to his feet and his sticks fell to the ground. This crippled man was standing, his hands raised in the air, the light of Heaven on his face, and he was giving glory to Jesus, just praising God with all his heart. I looked at him and said, 'You're healed. Come on out to the front!' When he was halfway across the floor, I said, 'Go back and get your sticks, and throw them on the platform.' Then I turned to the crowds and said, 'What this man has done, you can do! Every cripple, every person who is walking with crutches or sticks, you're healed, if you will get up and walk. Don't think about the pain or the accident or your broken leg – only think about Jesus, only see Jesus! Get up and walk!' And many, many people came, every one of them healed, until we had a pile of crutches on the platform. Why? Because for the first time they didn't look at their pain or their circumstances. They were looking at Jesus!

Peter was like that. He didn't see the storm, he didn't realise it was impossible. Why didn't somebody shout, 'Peter, you can't walk on water. You can't do it – don't do it!'? Peter stepped out in the storm. It was totally impossible, but he did it! Why did he do it? Was it because he was impetuous, acting before he realised the danger? Was it because, of all the disciples in the boat, only he had recognised Jesus in the darkness? Or was it that for a moment the Holy Spirit had 'seeded' a gift of faith, a kind of 'blind' faith, in his heart?

All the time his eyes were fixed on Jesus, there was no problem – he was walking, he was looking and he could see Jesus. The waves were there and the wind was behind him, but he was looking and he could see Jesus. There was no fear – it was a miracle. Interestingly, at this moment the stormy waves had become safer than the fragile security of the boat with the other disciples in it! Then suddenly, he looked down, saw the water, heard the wind, and when he took his eyes off Jesus, he began to sink. Miracles will happen in your life, but don't take your eyes off Jesus, don't look at the devil. Keep your eyes on Jesus and all the time your eyes are on Him you'll never sink, you'll never go down – that's the first miracle!

When Peter began to sink below the water he cried out, 'Lord, save me,' and in that exact moment, Jesus reached out His hand and lifted him. Even if for a moment you're sinking, you've taken your eyes off Jesus in the middle of your miracle, Jesus will lift you – every time – if you cry out, 'Jesus, help me.' That's the second miracle!

You may need Jesus like you've never needed Him before, but He is walking towards you to deliver you right now. Yours is the responsibility to cry out to Him, to ask Him to call you out of your crisis, then to step out of it into the security of His arms!

CHAPTER TWENTY

POSSESS THE BLESSINGS!

Moses was a great leader who brought the children of Israel out of slavery in Egypt to the edge of the Promised Land, and he commanded the people, 'The Lord your God has given you this land to possess it. Go in armed, all that are ready for war!' (Deuteronomy 3:18).

The children of Israel were just like you, and God uses them as an illustration in your life, of what is to happen to you. They had been travelling in a barren wilderness, but God gave them a wonderful promise, that they were going to enter a land full of blessing. They had to possess it, take it – all the blessings and promises of God – but first they had to see it, second they had to fight for it, and last they had to possess it!

When you repent and find Christ, there's a great excitement. I was eight years old when I found Christ. I got out of bed, knelt on the floor and said, 'Jesus, I want You. Come into my heart, my life and forgive my sin!' It was a miracle! I got back into bed and went straight to sleep! Next morning I JUMPED out of bed. I had a new life, I belonged to Jesus! I drew back the curtains and the whole world outside had changed! The trees were a brighter green, the birds sang as they'd never sung before, the sky was a more beautiful blue! It was many years before I found the truth: it wasn't the world that had changed that day; I had! I was born again – into a new life and a whole new excitement. And that was only the beginning.

But some people never go beyond the beginning.

A young couple came to their pastor and the husband said, 'I have a problem. I have to look after my young brother.' The pastor said, 'That's not a problem!' The husband replied, 'Oh, but it is! He's 30 years old but he's just like a baby – he's never grown up, he can't speak or walk or feed himself.' There are some of us who have been Christians for five, ten, twenty years but have never 'grown up'! It's not just the beginning that counts. We've got to move on with God, grow up, get to know Him – and possess the blessings of God!

I remember a little boy who was always falling out of bed. There would be a bang on the bedroom floor, his mother would pick him up and put him back, but after he had been in bed a while, there would be another big bang! So she asked, 'Why do you always fall out of bed?' He thought, then said, 'I fall out, because when I get in, I stay too near the getting-in side!' Some Christians are always 'falling out of bed' spiritually because they stay too near to the getting-in side! You must go right in and possess fully all the new life and blessings of God in Christ. Getting saved, the forgiveness of sin – that's just the beginning. There's so much more in this new life to possess.

The Bible is so rich, so full of promises. I want you to eat the Bible like you eat breakfast or lunch – take, eat, live the Word of God! It's the Bread of Life and it's more important than food. Jesus said that man cannot live by bread alone, but by the Word of God (Luke 4:4). I can fast, I can pray, but I can't do without the Word of God.

We should possess all the blessings of God, not part. But in order to do so, you need to see them for yourself and know what they are. Don't be like the children of Israel who came out of Egypt, then stopped at the edge of the Promised Land! Moses sent in twelve men to see what the land was like, how good it was, and they agreed that they saw the same things: a wonderful land, plenty of water, lots of milk, honey, and grapes SO BIG – everything bigger and better and more beautiful than you can imagine! But they had an argument. Ten of the men had no faith and said, 'It's impossible. Look at all the power the devil's got – big armies, big tanks, aeroplanes – even the men are bigger than we are! We can't do it.' Two of them said by faith, 'With God nothing is impossible. If God is with us, by faith we CAN go in and we CAN possess that land!' (Deuteronomy 13).

We can look at other believers and think, 'What a wonderful life they have. If only I could be like them!' Don't say, 'It's all right for you, but I can't do it. I'm too poor, too weak. It's impossible.' If God is with you, nothing is impossible. You just need a little faith. You CAN enter into that reality and it's far more wonderful than anything you can imagine, but it requires faith in God to enter and possess it for yourself. Yes, God's promised land IS wonderful, and available for you to possess in THIS life, not merely when you die. You can call on the Lord and be healed, you can be filled with the Holy Spirit, you can have so much power. For the real believer it is the most wonderful life – so full of the joy and the glory of God, you will never want to go back to the old way.

In May 2002, God gave me the vision of what He wanted me to do in Russia. I announced, 'We're not going to preach to just 10,000 people any more. We're going to reach more than a million every time.' Some said, 'You don't have enough money; you can't do it!'

But with God it IS possible. I believed God, and He's done it! Thank you, Father, because You did what You said, You did not fail me!

We have to look into the Word of God – we have got to SEE this land before we enter it. How can you take the blessing if you don't know what it is? How can you live the life of God if you don't know what that life is? How can you speak with tongues, prophesy, heal the sick without the gift of the Holy Spirit? How can we receive the Holy Spirit without first seeing it in the Word of God? Eat your Bible for breakfast, for lunch, and when you've got no food in the house you will never go hungry because God your Father has promised you His Bread every day! Do you KNOW the promises of God? Have you SEEN the promises of God? Before you read the Bible say, 'Lord, open my eyes. I want to see it and take it.'

But you have to fight for it, believe it and take it. The devil will always try to stop you receiving what God has for you. He will blind your eyes, deceive you that you are not good enough, bring every hindrance in your way. Moses said, 'Go armed and ready for war!' Yes, we have to fight today, not against God, but against all the powers of darkness, against every lying and deceiving spirit which will attempt to stop us receiving our promised blessings in Christ. When I wanted the baptism of the Holy Spirit with fire, I had to fight against the discouragement I received from other 'believers', but when I finally received, the fire was greater than I had expected. When I had cancer in my throat and asked God for healing, the devil said it was impossible. I fought unbelief and doubt so that when the answer came, it was an even greater miracle than I had asked for. When I was in prison for Bible smuggling, I fought against the demons of despair, fear, unbelief, and when the final answer came, it was many times greater than I had imagined in my wildest dream.

Once I visited an old man in a filthy little house. He had no wife, no children, no money, no food and I thought he was the poorest man in town. But I discovered this man had money in every bank, investments in gold mines, in oil – so much – yet he lived in poverty! The money was in the bank, in the investments, but he didn't enjoy it. He had nothing, yet he was rich beyond my dreams. So many Christians live like that: in poverty, always sick, always miserable. But your Father owns all the wealth in the world. He has promised you miracles of healing, power, joy unspeakable. Live in the joy of your inheritance, possess it now. It's yours through Christ. But you've got to take it by faith!

YOU have power over every evil spirit, every sickness, every difficulty – every one of you. When the devil comes, call upon the Name of Jesus! When you are weak in your body, in the Name of Jesus be strong! When you are sick, in the Name of Jesus be healed! Receive your promises NOW!

Isaiah 43:19 says: 'Behold I do a new thing, now it shall spring forth. I will even make a way in the wilderness and rivers in the desert.' God is doing a new thing in my life, and whether you are an old believer or a new-born believer, just one day old, God can do a new thing in YOUR life.

CHAPTER TWENTY-ONE

THE MARK OF FAITH

The theme and the title of all my TV programmes and evangelistic campaigns in Europe, Russia and Ukraine is the *Power of Faith in Jesus Christ*.

Faith in Jesus Christ is the key to release the power of God in your life. Not enough people use this key to the power and the glory of God.

1 Peter 1:7 says that the trial of your faith, which is much more precious than gold that perishes, though it is tested with fire, will be a praise, honour and glory at the appearing of Jesus Christ. So that just as gold has to be tested by fire, so FAITH has to be TESTED to prove its authenticity. Verse 5 says that we are kept by the power of God through FAITH unto a salvation which is to be revealed.

There is a great salvation which is to be revealed in the future – we only have part of that salvation here. We will only experience the real glory of God when we get into Heaven itself. But we have the beginning of that salvation now, enough to take us into the Kingdom. Please understand: we only experience the real glory and power of God when we are with Jesus. But we have enough power now to get us there. It's like sending a rocket into space: when the rocket is fired and leaves the earth, you cannot add any fuel to it – it has to have enough energy when it blasts off, to escape all the pull of gravity and get up there. The moment we receive salvation God puts His 'fuel', His energy and power, into us. His power is so explosive, every born-again man, woman and child becomes like a rocket with enough power to blast through all the power of the devil, into Heaven!

1 Peter 1:5 says that you are kept by this power, this energy of God, through FAITH, unto salvation. This means that from the moment you are saved, God puts enough spiritual energy in YOU to blast you through all the power of Satan – everything that can stop you – to take YOU into the Kingdom of God. How does this happen? Through faith! FAITH is the energy in you. FAITH is the driving power, the force, but not the motivation – that is something else, in your heart, between you and God. When you have the right motivation, faith becomes the driving power to fulfil it. When your motivation is ONLY for the fulfilment of God's purposes, you can ask God for the gift of faith, because faith is something which does not occur naturally in you; it is a gift from God, something given from outside, like fuel, put into you to fulfil God's purposes.

In verse 7 Peter says simply that faith is only faith when it is tested. Faith is not something in your mind – it's not something intellectual – it's a gift from God. It cannot be made or produced by man. But it is only real faith when it's tested. It's not always the devil who is testing your faith – God also tests your faith. It's too easy to say everything is the fault of the devil, but it's not true. God tests us, He's doing it all the time. But He's put a power in us that is strong enough to take us through all these hard testings into the Kingdom of God.

Where are you without faith? God wants this power in the church. Jesus performed many miracles of healing, but this is what He said to His disciples: 'You see all the things that I have done? You're going to be able to do these same things that I do, AND MORE!' Greater miracles, bigger miracles! So we should expect to see more miracles than Jesus saw. How? Through the Holy Spirit. We don't do it in our own power; it's the power of the Holy Spirit in us.

Faith is more valuable than gold (verse 7). Gold will perish, but faith will not. The Bible says that when Jesus comes back, the first thing He will see is our faith. It is our faith that will identify us; it's our faith that He will recognise.

The more I read the Bible, the more convinced I am that the most important thing after our salvation, is our relationship with Jesus Christ. And how can we define or explain this relationship we have with Jesus Christ? I've never seen Him, you've never seen Him, so how can we explain our relationship with Him? I believe that there is one factor more than anything else which can define our relationship with Jesus Christ. It's not just our worship, not the length of our prayers, nor how much we read the Bible; it is the faith we have in Him, how much we trust Him! That is the only thing that clearly, unmistakably marks our relationship with Jesus Christ.

Even in a human setting, trust is one of the most important defining factors in the relationships we have with other people. In business, how can we deal with people we do not trust? In the marriage partnership, how long does it last when there is no trust between husband and wife? In fact, lack of trust will undermine even the greatest love between people. Faith in God is trust. Do you trust Him? Do you believe Him? If you love God enough you will trust Him whatever happens – in every trial or temptation, in sickness and in health, in poverty or in wealth. The list is endless, because He can never betray your trust! Only the life you live, your words and your actions, will be the test of how much you trust, and love, Him.

I knew that 2002 was going to be very difficult, so in the January I went away alone for a week to pray. At the end of that week I could only come to one conclusion as to what God was saying to me. He was saying that I needed more faith. I see many miracles, I've always seen miracles, but do I have the gift of healing? Do I have the gift of miracles? I don't know. Maybe I do. But there is one gift I want more than anything else, and that's the gift of faith. For more than 50 years, ever since I received the Holy Spirit, I've been asking God for the gift of more faith. My week of prayer had such an effect on me, it was as if God said that the year 2002 would be like flying in an aeroplane at about 3000 metres, opening the door and jumping out – without a parachute. That's the best description: jumping out without a parachute. Now you will understand what kind of a year 2002 was. Many times during the course of the year I had to jump out of this 'plane'. I like a bit of sport, but I wouldn't have the courage to jump from an aeroplane – I would be frightened if I just looked! Someone would have to come behind me when I was standing at the door, and push me!

That's what testing your faith is! It's trusting God enough to let Him push you out of the door without a parachute! Now maybe you don't want this faith, but I do. In my life I have had to jump out not once, but many times. And every time God rescued me before I got to the bottom. If you want to release the power of God in your life, then you've got to do it too – trust Him! With God nothing is impossible.

When we launched the first of our live-TV evangelistic crusades in Russia during October 2002, we had the equipment and the staff from Ukraine to do it. We knew we would need five cameras, extra equipment, eight staff. We arrived at the airport in Moscow, and there was only one cameraman and one camera! The director had been taken seriously ill and couldn't fly. We couldn't get the equipment from Ukraine where our studio is, and when we looked at what we were going to do, it was not that we didn't have the money, we simply didn't have the staff and equipment to broadcast. It was absolutely impossible! So we had to jump out of this aeroplane without a parachute! And God worked a most powerful miracle. We rented old Russian state TV equipment, a Russian state TV crew and, with the help of two of our own Russian staff who had never been involved in TV before, we went by faith and we did it! By the power of God. He made a way. In five days in two different cities we reached between five and six million people with the Gospel – 90 minutes' peak viewing time, worship, preaching, call to repentance, prayer for healing with actual miracles which happened during the live broadcast! Without the TV director, without the cameras, without the equipment we broadcast live, on peak-time TV! That is one of the biggest miracles I have seen. What I am telling you about faith, I actually have to put into action myself, or I fail God! God tests our faith.

But our God is the God of the impossible things, who cannot fail. Only we ourselves can fail.

However, it is important to get this final part right. Remember, *faith itself is not the motivation in our lives* (motivation is in our heart and comes from the goal or vision God gives us), but faith is the power to fulfil the motivation, because it directly links us to God Himself.

CHAPTER TWENTY-TWO

CRISIS MANAGEMENT

As believers, when we look at our nation and what is happening in the world today, we can become discouraged: if only revival would come, or we could evangelise, or there were more miracles . . .

In 1 Kings 18, Elijah was even more depressed: he thought that he was the only believer left in the whole of Israel; that the whole nation had turned away from God and were worshipping other gods. Yet he commanded the people to come together, called for God to work miracles and saw fire fall from Heaven!

What we desperately need today is that the same spirit which was on Elijah should come on us. Elijah was not perfect – he had more than one emotional breakdown, more than one major crisis in his life. In this significant eighteenth chapter, this was just one experience when he realised that, humanly speaking, there was no hope. In his despair he imagined the whole situation to be worse than it was, to be totally out of control: that this nation which, more than any other, had witnessed a God of miracles – had been delivered from Egypt by powerful signs and wonders, had been led through 40 years of wilderness into prosperity, had the finest spiritual leadership in history – was now so backslidden that they had all returned to the gods they worshipped before their deliverance from Egypt.

We are taught today that crisis management is failure; that we must avoid getting into such situations; that even admitting how serious things are is a denial of faith. Yet according to the Bible, God is a God of the crisis. Today we know that when God answers prayer, so often He does it at the last moment, the moment of real crisis. Those who listen to my ministry and those who work closely with me on staff know that, above all, I am a realist. When preaching the Gospel I warn the people that becoming a believer is not a form of escapism. You will still have problems in your life. The difference is that before your conversion you had to solve them alone – now you have Jesus with you.

One of my daughters, who is a nurse, was with me in the hospital when they were testing me for cancer. While I was speaking faith, she was the realist: 'Dad, listen to the doctors' verdict. You will not get your real miracle of healing unless they first confirm the reality of your cancer!'

Some people who read my magazine, Prophetic Vision, were concerned because I have warned readers about the reality of the European Union, now also about the reality of Islam. Why? Am I a prophet of doom? No – read on!

Elijah saw the situation in his nation in his day and yes, he was very concerned. The crisis he saw was reality: a nation not only rejecting God but, worse still, turning to a very evil form of idolatry. While admitting the crisis, he saw the power and ability of God to answer. Now the visionary became a man of decisive action.

Why did I first go to Russia 35 years ago? Because to

me, at that time, Russia was the most impossible nation to evangelise: communism threatened to overwhelm the world. That is why I wanted to go then, and that is why I go now, believing for the fulfilment of those prophecies which say that the last great revival will come from Russia and spread into the whole of Europe.

I once preached in a Siberian prison to all 1400 inmates, desperate men: 200 multiple murderers, 400 serious sex offenders and 800 even worse criminals. The commandant said he was an atheist; that God could not change these men; that I was wasting my time. But, faced with the crisis of this challenge, the Holy Spirit came on me and God transformed the prison that day. All 1400 criminals repented and 20 of those convicts are now pastors. Some of the best evangelists in Russia today were saved that day in that place!

When we face the challenges of this world, we need to pray that the spirit which was on Elijah would come on us. Yes, the EU is the last empire before the end of the age; yes, the Antichrist is about to be revealed; yes, maybe the four demons have been released from the Euphrates (Revelation 9:14); yes, Islam is a threat to every country in the world; yes, we are living in an apostate, ungodly generation; yes, neither politicians nor so-called spiritual leaders have the answer to our overwhelming problems . . . Crisis!

But the God of my Bible is a God of crisis management. His reaction to these problems, according to historical record, is to show His power, by signs and wonders and miracles! God has always raised up men in times of crisis – men like Moses and Elijah, or in more recent times John Wesley, whose preaching saved Britain from the horrors of the French Revolution, Evan Roberts in the Welsh revival,

Smith Wigglesworth and others. Elijah's God is alive today and will raise up men and women of faith – full of the Holy Ghost, believing that the day of miracles is not past – to deal with the challenge.

My God is the greatest and most powerful God in all the world and He is about to work the greatest miracles of all time. Yes, we are about to write the sequel to the Acts of the Apostles; we are about to see the fulfilment of the Book of Revelation. And let me shout this loud enough to wake even the dead and bring Elijah back: Jesus is coming soon! I want you to know that, as for me, I believe the Book – 'in the last days I will pour out My Spirit on all flesh says the Lord' (Joel 2:28). I personally am ready to go. I am fired up, filled up, powered up, on my feet, ticket and sword in my hand, ready to go now. No power on earth or from hell can stop me. I'm not too old, too poor, too tired, too weak or ready to quit! If God could use Moses, David, Elijah, He can use me. I have the same Holy Spirit power they had, I believe in the same God, and I am already filled with revival fire. No more waiting – the urgency of the crisis alone is call enough. I have already seen the power of God in action, received a ten-fold more powerful anointing, preached the Gospel, won the lost and dying, healed the sick . . .

God challenged the people through Elijah: 'How long will you halt between two opinions? If the Lord is the true God, follow Him, serve Him, obey Him. But if these false gods are real, follow them!' (1 Kings 18:21).

Elijah said that you cannot sit on the fence! You will fall to one side or the other. That's exactly the situation we're in spiritually today. Everybody has to make a decision. If you don't, you fall off the fence and the decision is made for you. If you do not actively believe the Lord God, you will end up believing the lies of the devil.

Elijah challenged the prophets of Baal who had taken over the spiritual leadership of the people: 'You pray to your god, but he can't see, he can't answer. There is no God there! I'll pray to my God, because I know Him and His power, and the God that ANSWERS [prayer], He is the real God!' The spiritual crisis we are in now is the crisis moment when God is challenging spiritual leaders to test the reality of their own experience.

Just knowing that there is a God is not enough – even the devil knows and can quote the words of Scripture better than many (Luke 4). You need to be like Elijah and know who God really is, and how He reacts. If the situation is as bad as we are prophesying, don't panic, act in faith!

Elijah gave a challenge to the false prophets: 'You prepare a sacrifice, pray, and ask your god to send fire.' They spent all day, but their god did not answer. When evening came, Elijah prepared a sacrifice, but can Elijah's God answer? Before he even began to pray, he commanded his men to dig a big trench right round the sacrifice, then pour twelve barrels of water over it. What was Elijah doing? First, he had challenged the prophets of Baal, and they failed to get an answer to their prayer. Now he was calling on God to send fire, which would take a miracle, but before he prayed he himself made the answer to his prayer absolutely impossible by putting water where he needed fire!

We must get back to the authority of the Bible. When God answers, He does it by a miracle. The only real evidence of the reality of God that I find in my Bible is the miraculous. At this point, if Elijah does not believe in a God of miracles who can do things which are absolutely impossible, he is a dead man! If the prophets of Baal don't get him, King Ahab will, or worse still, Jezebel! If you do not believe in a God of miracles, you will not get an answer. As Elijah said to the people, choose today which kind of God you will serve! The challenge is even more necessary in our day: dead god or living powerful God? You are the one who must choose.

When Elijah asked the people, 'Are you for God or against Him?' they didn't answer yes or no, they just sat in the middle. But we need to demonstrate in our lives what God can do. It only took one man, Elijah, to demonstrate the power of God to a whole nation. I challenge you: let's call upon the power of God! Let's believe God like Elijah did! Let's rise up and do something in Jesus' Name! We need to get baptised with the Holy Ghost and fire!

Elijah called down fire from Heaven and it came on the sacrifice. If you today are not Elijah, at least be the sacrifice on God's altar. Oh God, send the fire! We are waiting and expecting you to answer, now!

CHAPTER TWENTY-THREE

MY 'MOUNTAIN' WAS LUNG CANCER

In December 2002, as part of the process of getting a resident's permit in Ukraine, I had to have a lung X-ray in order to prove I did not have TB, which is endemic out there. But the doctors called me back, took more X-rays, and then told me I had a shadow on my lung and that I had pneumonia. Probably I had already had it for over a month, because I remember a fever had started on the last day of October while I was evangelising in Siberia.

Back in England I was treated with antibiotics, but after two courses of treatment I went again for X-rays and the patch on my lung was bigger. The doctors became extremely worried. They didn't want me to travel overseas and they set up exhaustive tests in a hurry. They said bluntly, 'It's not pneumonia. You have lung cancer.'

I prayed about it, and I did go overseas to carry out my ministry, but the day after I got back the hospital process started. On the Thursday I had the CT (computer tomography) scan and it showed the cancer.

I believe in prayer and in a God of miracles. But I am faced with a challenge: do I really believe God or not? On the following Monday I had to go for a bronchoscopy, when they would put a camera down my lung and take a sample of the growth. The doctors had already fast-tracked me into a process which would lead to an operation to remove all or part of my right lung and on the Wednesday I was booked to go in for the final verdict. The only question was how much of my lung they would take away.

I said, 'Lord, how can I go back into Russia and preach like I preach and say that You are a mighty God of miracles who's got power to do everything, including heal cancer, if I have got half of my right lung cut out, followed by chemotherapy? If You have finished with me, if my ministry is over, then don't heal me, because if I can no longer evangelise I might as well die. I have no other reason to live. But if You want me to go back into Russia and Ukraine and finish the work You gave me to do, then I want You to heal me completely!' But I only had a few days, from Thursday to Monday!

God said to me, 'David, you've got a mountain in your life that you've got to move, and that mountain is to get that cancer out from your lung. If you can believe that without an operation you can be completely healed, then nothing will be impossible from there on.' Now desperately seeking God's answer from Scripture, I was reading from Jeremiah 33:6, 'I will bring health and healing'; and Jeremiah 33:20–21, 'I will not break my covenant with David'; and Psalm 89:35, 'I will not lie to David'; and 'Is anything impossible with God?' (Jeremiah 32:17, 27).

On the Monday I was in the hospital, tubes down my lung looking for cancer, but God had already given me the answer. I knew it was gone. The doctors looked at me in amazement and said, 'You have no cancer!'

I didn't go to a healing evangelist, I went to the Word of God and God completely healed me. No operation, no treatment – I only had God and the Bible, and that's all I needed to confound the doctors. They were shocked, they didn't believe God. But I do, I believe in a God of power, of miracles.

The Bible is very clear. Isaiah 53:5 says that Jesus was wounded for our sin, bruised for our iniquity and with His stripes we are healed. Matthew 8:16–17 says that Jesus healed all who were sick to fulfil what was spoken by the prophet Isaiah. So healing is to fulfil Bible prophecy! I talk about Bible prophecy, I write about it in *Prophetic Vision* magazine, but part of Bible prophecy is healing the sick. I believe Bible prophecy. Some people say that healing was only for the time of Jesus. But this prophecy is not ended. Jesus only healed for three years. There are more miracles of healing today than at any time in the history of the church – all over the world. Today in Russia this is how we are showing the glory of God, live on TV – seeing big miracles, every time I preach the Gospel!

Talking of the last days in Matthew 24:14 Jesus says: 'This Gospel shall be preached in all the world for a witness to the nations, and then shall the end come.' Jesus did not say there will be a worldwide revival. He said that the preaching of the Gospel will be a witness to all nations, a demonstration to the whole world. My responsibility before God is not only to preach the Gospel, but to demonstrate the power of our God with authority. We have power in the Holy Ghost and we have authority in the Name of Jesus. Today God needs preachers who know His power and authority. I have learnt to receive authority from

God and to act in power. Why? So that until Jesus comes back I can be a witness of the glory of God to a world that doesn't know Him.

CHAPTER TWENTY-FOUR

POWER COMES WITH REALITY

Looking back, 2003 was without question the hardest year of my life!

It began with the diagnosis of my lung cancer in January. Then after my miraculous healing in February, by March the schedule of broadcasting the crusades live on TV precipitated an enormous financial crisis. It feels as if I went through a whole lifetime in just one year, but through it God proved to be so powerful and worked so miraculously, it seemed as though I had started a whole new life. Yet I'm still only on the edge of the power God is about to manifest!

In 2004 God gave me a new challenge, greater than in 2003!

I don't preach an easy Gospel. Yes, I preach the Gospel, about the power and the glory of Jesus Christ, Son of the living God! But in Deuteronomy 4, Moses warned the people first that they must go in and possess the Promised Land, but then (verses 26–27), once they were in, he said,

'You're going to go through difficulty and trial.' When I preach the Gospel, I am a realist. I do not tell people that coming to Christ is suddenly an end to all their problems, everything will be transformed, living on cloud nine, twanging a harp! Let's be realistic: the church is called into battle to fight for the Kingdom! Yes, me as an evangelist winning people for Christ, but also you, like me, fighting for those things which are our right to possess, like healing and deliverance. We're at war with an enemy who is fighting to prevent us possessing. I hate the devil, and I fight him by demonstrating the power of God. You must fight him, not allow him to stop you receiving. Some look to the church for ceremony, for a formula, for peace, but I find God most, not in the calm, but in the reality of my life. I discovered a long time ago that the most important thing which creates character is not WHAT happens to us so much as OUR REACTION.

Moses encourages the people in verse 27, 'If from where you are . . . you will seek the Lord your God, you WILL find Him, if you seek Him with ALL your heart.' So, in the midst of every distress, fear, want, even sickness – whatever situation you are in – there you will find God. So often we are told that if you want to find God, you've got to be 'holy', to give up everything, separate yourself, shut yourself up like in a monastery. No, the reality is that spirituality is not isolating yourself, not trying to be some kind of 'holy' person – it's YOU dealing with GOD right where you are. If you want to meet with God, you don't have to wait until you have done this or that. I would never have become an evangelist, never seen a miracle of healing, if God had waited until I was perfect before He answered my prayers. I call on God, He deals with me where I am.

That's why I was healed. Not because I was 'holy'. What God looks at is the deep desire of your heart.

I was asked recently, 'How many hours a day do you pray? How much do you read the Bible?' The truth is, there are some days when I can hardly pray, because I'm tired, exhausted, I'm travelling. If I'm coming from Siberia, there are 36 hours in my day! Even the young men find it difficult to keep up with my punishing travelling/preaching schedule. Yes, believe me, when I'm in a crisis, I do fast and pray! But in some crises when I'm travelling and ministering, I just can't fast – but God is right there in my crisis. We've got to search for God and find Him right where we are. If you think my life as an evangelist is easy, I can disillusion you. Some people say they want to be like me, but if they knew the truth, they wouldn't want to. When I had the lung cancer I had a very busy schedule – don't ask me how much I fasted, how much I prayed. When you know you have only a short time to live, you learn how to pray! I said, 'Lord, I cannot go back into Russia and talk about a God of miracles and power if I've had my lung taken out!' Yes, with the power of the Holy Ghost in me, I could be strong and do it, but I said, 'I cannot stand up and boast about the God who can do anything, who can work miracles, and admit I've had one lung removed!' You see, I don't preach, I BOAST about my God. He's the greatest, the most powerful.

I am very PROUD of my God!

By my bed I keep my praying Bible, where God talks to me and I talk to God. When I had the cancer I would wake up troubled in the night, pick up my praying Bible and God would speak to me, comfort me, and I would go back to sleep. I used to say, 'If You've finished with me, just tell me. But if You have a whole new life in front of me and want me to get back out there in Russia, with a new power and a new anointing, to see things I've never seen before, then I want You to answer me and heal me. I haven't seen Your real power and Your glory yet, and if you will let me see it, Lord, I want You to work a miracle.' And He did!

We have a covenant relationship with God. It's not simply based on our faith, which is weak and can fail, but a covenant which cannot fail or be broken. When you come to Christ, you enter into a covenant relationship with God, signed and sealed by the blood of Christ. God separates you from the guilt AND the power of sin. You are delivered from Satan and all his works – not when you get to Heaven, but down here, in your crisis, in your distress, in all the trouble the devil puts upon you. Whoever you are, whatever you are, you are delivered by the power of the blood. It's an unbreakable covenant to defeat the power of the devil in your life.

Yes, we make mistakes, we fail, we fall. But He cannot fail us. The Bible reminds us that God came to deliver the sinner, not the righteous. None of us can enter the Kingdom of God through our own righteousness, so we cannot 'earn' the answers to prayer through our 'holiness'. God did not heal my cancer because of my 'holiness', but because He is God!

This is what Moses was saying to the people: don't look at the troubles, at the difficulties, at your sickness, your poverty. Look at God and you'll find Him, if you do it with all your heart. I make a lot of mistakes, but I LOVE Him so much!

How do you recognise God? How do you find Him? What is the evidence of God's existence in the Bible? It's the fact that He's a God of miracles, who answers prayer when it takes a miracle. This is the reality. This is the God we're looking for: a God who answers all who call on Him, by miracles, by signs, by wonders. This is the evidence! Take the miraculous out and you destroy the reality of who God is. You make Him no different from men!

Moses says, in Deuteronomy 4:32, 'Ask now of the days that are past, since the day God created man on the earth, and ask from one side of Heaven to the other, whether there has been any such great thing as this thing is.' He challenges the people to ask the question in two dimensions: in time from creation until now, and in space from one side of the world to the other: 'Have you ever seen a miracle as great as this that God did when He delivered Israel out of Egypt – by miracles, by signs and by wonders?'

In the Bible God uses miracles to demonstrate who He is. The greatest spiritual revivals in history have been demonstrated by the miraculous

In these last days God is saying to the church, NOW, 'I am prepared to do something greater, bigger, more miraculous than anything that has ever been seen before in the earth or in the church.' God is about to do the greatest miracles the world has ever seen. He's going to raise up men like Elijah; men with an anointing to do greater works than Jesus did (John 14:12)! Why? Because we are living in the days of the return of Christ, when we're going to see revival fire bursting on the church, until we are working and believing and moving into spiritual victory – all in the preparation for the glorious return of Jesus. People will ask, 'Has anybody ever seen or heard anything like this before?'

God is moving today by the Holy Spirit, but we haven't yet seen the REAL glory of God, what He CAN do. But it WILL come! Yes, before Christ comes, in my lifetime, God is going to reveal His glory on earth. I'm determined to see it.

Part IV

Miracles Demonstrate God's Power

CHAPTER TWENTY-FIVE

ARE THESE MIRACLE HEALINGS REAL? IF SO, WHY?

When people hear about the miracles God is doing in Russia and Ukraine, they ask me, 'Are these miracle healings real? And if so, why?'

The answer to the first question is emphatically 'Yes, they are real!' For the second question – why do they happen? – the answer in this chapter is brief. The matter is dealt with more fully in my earlier book, *Why Siberia?*, which answers the question as to why these miracles happened so powerfully in that remote part of Russia. However, I will briefly answer the question by giving here three strong reasons why: (i) because in Siberia and in Ukraine we are moving in a strong anointing of the Holy Spirit, which is bringing revival; (ii) because this is the way in which God is demonstrating His power to these nations who were taught that either there was no God, or if there was, that they did not need Him; (iii) because of what God has revealed to me personally, and which I will show you.

Before you read further, let me remind you that not only have I seen and recorded tens of thousands of healings under my ministry, but I have experienced two outstanding personal miracles of healing from cancer, both confirmed medically. In 1964 I was healed of cancer on my vocal cord and in 2003 I was healed of cancer in my right lung!

In answering both questions, I would suggest that there are two separate ministries of healing outlined in Scripture: healing within the church and healing under the evangelist. This explains the different authorities and commands we have and the reason why I believe that although the ministries may function separately, they are complementary and not contradictory. The Bible gives us four separate authorities for healing: the promise of Isaiah 53 and other related scriptures, the commands of Jesus, the gifts of the Holy Spirit, and, interestingly, the fulfilment of prophecy.

Physical healing is an integral part of the atonement. It has been bought for us, together with our salvation, through Christ's suffering and death. Isaiah 53 states clearly that 'He was wounded for our transgressions . . . And with His stripes we are healed.' We all believe that our sin was taken away and the penalty was paid by Christ's suffering and death. We do not question our salvation, which is by faith in the finished work of Christ's atonement. However, the Bible clearly states that not only our sin but also our sickness was borne by Him. We need to apply the same level of faith to our deliverance from sickness as we do to our deliverance from sin.

It is true that many times people come to me as an evangelist simply because they lack the real assurance of salvation – not the teaching, but the faith to apply it. Some have questioned why, when the call is made for those who want to repent to come forward, some people come a second time. I welcome this if, on the previous occasion, they had not fully experienced that deep conviction of reality brought by the Holy Spirit, but now the miracle has happened.

If you question that the scripture I referred to in Isaiah 53 is merely an Old Testament prophecy, referring only to a full salvation from sin, let me remind you that in the New Testament it is used as a reference to healing rather than salvation. Matthew 8:16–17 says Jesus 'healed all who were sick, that it might be fulfilled which was spoken by Isaiah the prophet, saying, Himself took our infirmities, and bore our sicknesses'. So the healing ministry of Christ was clearly seen as a fulfilment of Isaiah's prophecy, and it still is for today – just as much as salvation from sin – because both were fulfilled literally through Christ's suffering and death. Hence healing fulfils both Scripture and Bible prophecy.

I grew up in the tradition that, in dealing with 'divine healing', as we used to call it, we had to 'pray' for the sick. Having seen over the whole period of my ministry some outstanding miraculous healings, including my own two healings from cancer and one of my daughter's from meningitis, I believe very strongly in the healing power of Christ. And over these last years working in Russia and Ukraine, I have been more challenged than ever.

In 1992 I was speaking to crowds of more than 10,000 in Mayaki, a village near Odessa, when the pastor asked me to go to another small town where there was no church, no Bibles and they had never even heard the name Jesus! The hall was packed with about 800 people, almost all of whom accepted Christ after I had preached the Gospel to them. However, I was concerned that in their new belief they actually needed a practical demonstration of who Jesus really is. For the first time in my life I said simply but boldly to the crowd, 'I can prove that Jesus is alive. If all the sick will come forward, I will put my hands on them in the Name of Jesus. If He is not alive no one will be healed, but if He is, then miracles will happen, because I will heal you in His Name.' I was shocked by my own boldness! Tradition says that I must tell them, 'I will PRAY for you,' and then apologise and say, 'I cannot heal you, only Jesus can.' But before the meeting, I had been reading the words of Jesus in Luke 9:1–2 and 10:8–9, where He calls first twelve then seventy disciples and COMMANDS them to preach the Gospel and HEAL the sick – not 'pray' for them. Later I found that Matthew 10:1–8 is even stronger than Luke.

In the meeting that day hundreds came forward, and we recorded that almost every sick person was healed when I obeyed HIM in FAITH. Since then I have studied the commands of Christ to His disciples regarding healing and I cannot find one place in the four Gospels where Jesus ever tells His disciples to 'pray' for the sick. He always says either HEAL them or lay hands on them, as in Mark 16:17–18, where He says, 'These signs will follow those who believe . . . they shall lay hands on the sick and they shall recover.'

So where does the tradition of 'praying' come from? The main reference usually quoted is in James 5:14, 'Is any sick among you? Let him call for the elders of the church; and let them pray over him, anointing him with oil in the Name of the Lord: and the prayer of faith shall save the sick.' This is for the believers in the church, the ministry within the 'body'. It clearly calls for the 'elders', the oil, praying in faith and forgiveness within the church.

All the other references in the Gospels, where Jesus is

speaking, must be for the evangelist, as every reference in the commands of Jesus is to the disciples, not to the church, which did not come into existence until Pentecost, and He always says, 'Preach the Gospel . . . HEAL the sick.'

In order to demonstrate to unbelievers that Jesus is alive and to uplift and glorify the Name of Jesus we need to preach under a strong anointing of faith by the Holy Spirit, which will bring signs, wonders, miracles and healings. We must have evangelism with power and fire to bring real confirmation of the truth we preach.

And in order to do this, we need two extremely important things: power AND authority. We know that the power is through the Holy Spirit, but the authority?

We hear so much about anointing and power, but very little about the believer's authority. So many sense, correctly, the need for power in healing, knowing that the power is through the baptism and anointing of the Holy Spirit. But then I see and hear them shouting, supposedly to demonstrate that power – or more often praying long prayers, especially in tongues.

But we have AUTHORITY over demons and sickness!

In the natural order of command in the world, those with REAL authority don't shout. Usually those who do shout don't have the authority. Look at the Scripture. It says in Matthew 8:16, 'He cast out spirits with His WORD and healed all who were sick.' I believe that although I have had a ministry of healing throughout my life, it is only since finding this authority that the present, more powerful, anointing has come.

When the centurion came to Jesus in Matthew 8:5–10, he said, 'I am not worthy that You should enter my house . . . but I am a man under authority. I say to my servant go and he goes.' The centurion had AUTHORITY to COMMAND obedience. And he recognised this same authority in Jesus to command, when he said to Him, 'Speak the word only and my servant will be healed.' This is exactly what Jesus meant when, in Luke 9:1, He gave His disciples 'power and authority over all demons and to heal diseases'.

The centurion recognised authority and demonstrated such great FAITH in Jesus and in His authority, it was enough even to heal his servant with one word! This is the secret of power over sickness and evil – authority – and I believe that we have this same authority that Jesus had. Look at Matthew 10:1 where He gave His disciples authority to cast out unclean spirits and heal all manner of sickness and disease, and at verses 7–8 where He says to them, 'Preach . . . Heal the sick . . . Raise the dead!' If we want to heal the sick we need boldness and authority to cast out the sickness.

Let me warn you that we cannot really understand or receive this authority unless we fully know and understand the ONE from whom we would receive it. Remember that authority is in two directions: I have authority in my ministry directly from God Himself through the command of His Word, then I exercise this God-given authority when I preach the Gospel and when I heal the sick, so that I can command the sickness to go in the Name of Jesus, and command the sinner to repent.

We also need faith. In Matthew 17:20, Jesus said that if we have FAITH as a grain of mustard seed, we will speak to a mountain and COMMAND it to move. Command is authority, but FAITH is one of the GIFTS of the Holy Spirit. This is where the importance of prayer comes into the healing ministry, because Jesus clearly says in verse 21, 'This kind goes not out but by prayer and fasting.' I believe very strongly that the gifts and anointing are dependent on prayer AND fasting.

In 1 Corinthians 12:9, we read that one of the nine gifts of the Holy Spirit is the 'gift of healings', and in verses 28 and 29, in the ministry of the church, we read that God has put 'workers of miracles' and 'gifts of healings'. So healing is both a gift of the Holy Spirit and a ministry within the church. Alongside this must be seen another powerful gift, the gift of faith, so that what we need, we can receive by faith. These gifts do not come from man, but by the anointing and power of the Holy Spirit alone. This is why we must begin with prayer and fasting – first.

When we receive the Holy Spirit, we speak with tongues. Most believers who have received the Spirit do this without question, but do not go beyond, almost as if this is the only gift, or certainly the most important. I believe that these gifts are, according to Paul's writings, to be used regularly in the ministry in the church, but that as we grow spiritually we can increase in the gifts, and in the number of gifts we manifest. To me faith, the working of miracles and gifts of healing are far more important gifts than merely speaking with tongues. Paul says, 'Covet the best gifts,' but in your life this is one of the spiritual decisions you must make, as to which you ask for. Even after more than 50 years of ministry, I still regard faith as being the most important gift in my life, and still ask for more faith constantly. I will never have enough! However, please remember that these gifts and this anointing which you are told to 'covet' are only given to demonstrate the glory of God, not to bring glory to the user of the gifts.

There is much more that could be said concerning healing. Many books have been written on this subject. The arguments have raged over the centuries and will continue. Some attempt to excuse themselves by saying that healing and miracles are not for today. All I know is that they happen in my ministry and I have attempted to show from the Word of God why these miracles of healing are happening in Siberia and Ukraine, worldwide, NOW. This is not merely theory, but a demonstrable fact. IT HAS HAPPENED! IT IS HAPPENING! IT WILL GO ON HAPPENING UNTIL CHRIST HIMSELF RETURNS TO TAKE OVER FROM US AND COMPLETE THE WORK!

I experienced my own healing from cancer 40 years ago and two years ago, and I am experiencing it and seeing it with my own eyes in Russia and Ukraine today. The evidence is there, but it began in me as a teenager, when I had a hunger for God and began seeking Him for myself. Brought up in a godly family, I wanted the experimental evidence in my own life. What about you? Is God challenging your spiritual thinking, or do you have a personal need of healing? The answer is right before you. If I have not answered your questions, ask your Father. He knows more than I do. And remember that the Word says that Jesus is praying for you – right now!

CHAPTER TWENTY-SIX

CAN EVERYONE BE HEALED?

Doubt is one of the devil's biggest weapons against believers. Satan did not say to Eve in the garden, 'Eat those apples. God does not mind.' He sowed doubt: 'Did God say no?' Today he uses the same doubt to destroy God's authority and take us out of the blessing that God has given us. The following are actual questions people ask me.

Q. Not all who are prayed for are healed. Can God be equally glorified in Christians who are not healed?

A. Yes, He can, if that is what they really want! But it is not God's perfect will for them. God did not want Eve to doubt. She lived in God's paradise, but because she doubted God's word, she spent her life under the influence of evil and her son was murdered. But God in mercy provided a final redemption because He still loved her! I understand the problem in people's minds – we don't see everyone healed and it grieves me deeply – but this is the challenge which leads me to seek stronger faith to bring more healing, not to reject God's deliverance! When, aged 32, I had throat cancer the Lord challenged me: did I want the easy or the hard way? He said the easy way was to have the operation; the hard way was to fast, pray and believe until a miracle would happen. I deliberately asked God to take me the hard way!

In Psalm 115:17–18 David says, 'The dead praise not the Lord,' but we are seeking the praise and glory of God!

I want to tell you, Jesus commanded us to both preach the Gospel AND heal the sick (Luke 9:2). These two are inseparable. The healing of the sick is the demonstration of the Gospel – see Matthew 9:6 where Jesus said to the onlookers, 'But that you may know that the Son of man has power on earth to forgive sins.' He said to the sick of the palsy, 'Arise, take up your bed and walk.'

Q. Isn't sickness part of the cross we must carry?

A. The cross that Jesus carried was not sickness, but rejection, torture and death! The cross He asked us to carry is not sickness, but the persecution, hardship, rejection and even death that follow being His disciples and preaching His Gospel (Matthew 10:38; Mark 8:34; Luke 9:23; 14:27). Will you carry that cross? Then get rid of your sickness or you will never be fit to carry it! Jesus was no sick feeble Man, but the strongest, fittest Man who has ever lived! That must be your ideal.

Matthew 8:16–17 tells us that Jesus healed all who were sick, to fulfil that which was spoken by Isaiah the prophet, saying, 'Himself took our infirmities and bore our sicknesses.' So even at the time of the actual ministry of Jesus, the Bible says that Christ's atonement for our sin is also His atonement for sickness and disease; that the cross He carried was our healing. Why not carry that cross of healing (1 Peter 2:24; Isaiah 53)? Sin and sickness are not from God. Both come from the devil. The purpose of the first coming of Jesus was to make a way of escape from the evil which Satan and ultimately man, by his disobedience, brought into the world: 'For this purpose the Son of God was manifested, to destroy the works of the devil!' (1 John 3:8). However, this is only in part today. None of us is perfect in ourselves; we live in a world of sin and sickness and are surrounded by them. When Christ returns we shall be taken out of this world into the Kingdom of Heaven. Then there will be no more sin, sickness or death. Until then, walking by faith, we must overcome sin – and temptation – and sickness.

Q. Is my sickness God's punishment for my sin? Perhaps He is teaching me something.

A. If you think like that, you will not be healed. No, just as God forgives sin, instantly, He wants to heal you, NOW! God loves you! When Jesus healed the blind man the religious leaders asked, 'Who sinned, this man or his parents?' Jesus said that it was neither! If God were to punish us now for every sin or mistake, then every one of us would be dead, including me!

To say that our sickness is God's punishment for our sin denies the truth of the Bible, which says Christ has already paid the price of sin for us! It's the devil who brings sin and sickness into your life. God has made a provision in Christ to deal with both!

Q. How about those who are not healed, or who are healed and then lose their healing? Aren't you afraid they will be disappointed and lose their faith? Wouldn't it be better not to pray?

A. If I believed this, I would not even preach the Gospel! Almost every time I evangelise, there are those who reject and who then become harder to win. 'He that being often reproved hardens his neck, shall . . . be destroyed' (Proverbs 29:1).

I hear of so many who condemn evangelistic crusades because, of the thousands who come forward in the meetings to repent, not all come to the church and remain believers. Many go back into their sin. Jesus' answer to this was the parable of the sower: some seed fell on good ground, some fell among thorns and some were choked by weeds (Matthew 13:3–9). It is the same with healing: not all will be healed, and some may lose their healing. Not because this is God's way, but because the devil tempts them, or others deceive them into believing that 'it cannot last'. If they are told this enough times some will believe it! Also many are like nine of the ten lepers who were healed and will not even return to give thanks.

No, not everyone is healed, but this is not God's perfect will. It is even recorded of Jesus that in His own country 'He could do no mighty works because of their unbelief' (Matthew 13:58). Then in Matthew 17, when the disciples could not heal the epileptic boy, the father complained to Jesus, who instantly healed him. The disciples came to Jesus privately and asked, 'Why couldn't we heal him?' Jesus did not compromise. He said, 'Lack of faith!' Not on the part of the child, but the disciples. It does not take enormous faith to move mountains, but the child-like, seed-like faith of a simple believer. I know, because I have commanded 'mountains' and seen them move many times!

I once listened to criticism and as a result I became so discouraged I stopped organising big crusades and praying for the sick. Because of that, for some years I saw no one healed. Even today, after a meeting where I see the sick healed, I will often go home and grieve more over ones I didn't see healed (or who didn't repent) than I rejoice over the miracles I did see. It only drives me once more to fast and pray for more Holy Spirit power, to be more like Jesus in my ministry. Jesus preached the Gospel – so I do; Jesus healed the sick – so I do.

Smith Wigglesworth has gone down in history as a man of faith. Why? Because of the healing miracles. We need more like him in the church today. In the Bible Jesus said simply, 'Preach the Gospel, heal the sick.' In faith I believe it – I do it – I see it.

Surprisingly in the crusades in Russia I see many people healed who have absolutely no faith but who come in desperate need. God sees their desperation!

Q. Are you opposed to traditional medicine?

A. No, I'm not. There are wonderful Christian doctors. If I have a toothache, I go to the dentist; and yes I wear spectacles, but I have no eye disease and gradually God has restored my sight – I don't have bi-focal lenses and the lenses are so weak, the optician says that I can do without altogether. If I have a health problem, yes I visit the doctor. If he diagnoses a problem then I know what to pray for specifically. When I had the lung problem in 2002 I went to the doctor. At first I thought it was merely pneumonia, possibly through overwork and tiredness. When it did not clear up I returned to the doctor, who sent me to the hospital, where I had every kind of test. By that time I was bleeding through the nose and failed the breath test. However, one of my daughters, a qualified nurse, said, 'Have the X-ray and the CT scan. Until the doctors confirm that you have lung cancer you cannot prove the miracle of a God who can heal that cancer!' The cancer was confirmed, God healed me, and then the doctors confirmed that, without any treatment, my healing was a miracle! Out of interest, no one knows why I developed the cancer. I have never smoked or lived in a polluted atmosphere. One possibility could be that I have been into the villages affected by the Chernobyl explosion and even twice visited the actual power station itself, both filming and evangelising the workers there.

I believe that with God, prevention is better than cure and we should not abuse our bodies, which can cause sickness. Often when people come to me for healing I can recognise, without being a doctor, that their problem is due to a wrong lifestyle. If you smoke, you are likely to get lung cancer; if you put on very excessive weight, you run the risk of diabetes and heart problems. These are facts. Yes, God can heal you, but I recommend that a healthy diet can mean prevention rather than cure.

I love to see God heal people the doctors cannot help! To me, the real miracles of healing are when doctors have tried to heal and failed, then God takes over and by a miracle does what the most expert of doctors cannot do. I have seen many people healed of broken bones and the effects of accidents, especially young people, and many other young ones born blind, deaf, crippled, where medical science can do nothing.

I love to tell of the 22-year-old girl in Australia who was born with a spinal deformity and grew instantly 10 cm taller. And the young man in East Germany who had steel pins inserted into his right hip, knee and ankle, because of a motor accident. The miracle was, God literally melted the steel pins and he could kneel and squat and bend his joints freely! And the 22-year-old boy in a Russian hospital, dying from the effects of drug abuse, AIDS and gangrene in his right leg. They wanted to amputate his leg above the knee, but I knew he would die, because the AIDS had damaged his immune system. I told him not to have the operation; that God would heal him. I said, 'When I come to Perm next time, you and I will stand on the platform together and give glory to God for your healing!' Six months later I was back in Perm, holding a crusade live on TV to the whole region. On the first night I made an appeal to Anton via the TV broadcast to come and tell about his healing. Sure enough, on the next night, Anton was there on the platform with me to give glory to God just as I had told him he would! Anton had believed, refused the operation, and walked out of the hospital – healed! Now he is healed of AIDS, married, and in Bible school training to be an evangelist like me! That is the miracle of Russia: the hundreds of young people healed by a miracle but now serving God across the nation as evangelists and pastors. This is why we have revival there! Not my preaching, but God's miracles are the greatest testimony.

CHAPTER TWENTY-SEVEN

LIVE LIKE THIS!

Acts 3:1 says, 'Peter and John went up to the Temple . . . and a man, born lame, was carried who was laid daily at the Beautiful Gate of the Temple to ask money from those who entered . . . He saw Peter and John about to go into the Temple and asked money from them. Peter said, 'Look at us.' He expected to receive something from them but Peter said, 'I've no silver, no gold but what I have I give you. In the Name of Jesus Christ of Nazareth, rise up and walk,' and he took him by the right hand, lifted him up and immediately his feet and ankle bones received strength, and leaping up, stood and walked, and entered with them into the Temple walking and leaping and praising God.'

This crippled man was so happy. He was not miserable and certainly not religious. The power of Jesus had just healed him! He had a reason to rejoice, something to shout about. Jesus is the greatest – Jesus is the most wonderful person in the world! One minute this man was a cripple, the next minute by a miracle he was completely healed. What happened? Born a cripple, he couldn't walk, he couldn't run, he couldn't play football or fight with other boys, he couldn't go to school, he couldn't get a job, he couldn't get married . . . All he could do was sit outside the Temple and hope that somebody would give him money.

However, it was not Jesus Himself who came to help him. In the Bible by the time this miracle happened, Jesus was already dead, and now, resurrected, He was in Heaven, His earthly ministry finished. Please don't tell me that miracles could only happen when Jesus was alive! Jesus was gone, but the miracles were still happening. During His lifetime Jesus went to the Temple many times, and I'm certain that He actually saw this man who sat at the main entrance, the way He would usually enter, and He did not heal him! Now Jesus was gone, but the power to work miracles had not ended.

When Peter and John saw this man crying out, 'Money, money . . . I want money for food. I'm a poor cripple . . .' they said, 'We've got no money, but we've got something worth far more than money!' Peter reached out his hand, and this crippled man – more than 40 years old – leapt to his feet instantly! This miracle didn't take a week or a month. He didn't have to go to the hospital, he didn't go to the doctor. This was an instant miracle – it happened right there, at that moment. One minute he was crippled, the next minute Peter reached out his hand and the man jumped, walked, ran. It was a miracle! But not one directly performed by Jesus (if you understand). He was gone, but the miracles still continued because the power and authority had passed to His disciples.

Look where this crippled man – who had never walked, never worked, never married – is sitting. Behind him is the big Temple, the centre for all the religion in Jerusalem; in front of him just two simple fishermen, but men who know

Jesus personally. The power did not come out of the Temple, despite its splendour, nor out of its religious ceremonies, but out of Peter and John, ordinary men full of the Holy Spirit. This miracle happened in Acts 3, but chapter 4 says that as a direct result of this one healing miracle, 5000 new believers were added to the church. That's even more than the 3000 on the Day of Pentecost!

One book in the Bible is not yet finished. Every new convert, every person healed, every miracle that happens today, is a new page being added to the Acts of the Apostles, which you and I are still writing today!

I expect miracles to happen all the time and they do. Whenever I preach the Gospel, I call the sick people to come and I say, 'God will work miracles. I cannot heal your sickness, so don't look at me, look at God. The God of the Bible is alive and He's going to demonstrate this in front of you now. How? By a practical demonstration of a miracle, by mending broken bodies, broken marriages, broken homes, broken lives, by changing the alcoholic, the criminal, the drug addict – now!'

All over Russia, I've seen many criminals changed by a miracle. Once when I was visiting a prison in Siberia, a man came to me who had been in prison 24 years. Yet he was so happy. He was playing his guitar, singing and rejoicing. So I asked him, 'Why are you the happiest man in this prison?' He said, ' I was a murderer, but in here I found Jesus! The curse of the devil is broken. All my sin is gone. I'm in prison, but Jesus set me free! That's why I'm rejoicing. Thank God for the prison, because here I found Jesus – not religion – and He has changed my life!'

I met another man in Siberia and he was the happiest man in the crusade meeting. He was dancing for joy. I couldn't understand why until he told me, 'I've just come out of prison and there's two reasons I'm so happy. First, when I was in the prison someone told me about Jesus. He forgave every sin and changed my life! Second, I've only been out of prison for two weeks, but because they saw the change in me, everyone in my family has found Jesus and He's changed their lives too!'

I received a letter from a prisoner on death row in a Zambian prison which really touched my spirit. Joseph wrote, 'If everything goes according to the judge's verdict, I will be executed by hanging one day. I am an Angolan national and spent more than 15 years in the rebel Unita army. I was abducted and forced into the army as a boy aged 12, and have never met my parents. I came to know about God in an underground church in the rebel army camp. I repented and received Christ and His forgiveness. In this underground church I learned the most important thing: that murder is forbidden by God and is punishable by burning in the lake of fire after death. Because of the fear of hell, I fled to Zambia where, on reporting myself to the authorities, I was arrested and charged with all the forms of atrocities which the rebel army ever committed. While in prison, I came to know more about God through knowing Jesus. It appeared as if I had come to this prison and the death sentence in Zambia for the sake of knowing the true God. I have really benefited.'

Don't say, 'Oh, I believe, I believe . . .' when you don't really believe. CALL on Him, He will CHANGE your life, He will forgive your sin. THAT is the power of God!

But what happened to that cripple in the Bible? All he was thinking about when he saw Peter and John was money. But money couldn't change his life. Money alone cannot change your life either; no money in the world can buy peace with God. Only God can forgive every sin and only God can change your life. Only God can look at you, a miserable sinner, and say from His heart, 'I love you, I love you.' God wants to put His arms around you and say, 'I hate your sin, but I love you.' God hates sin, but He loves sinners. The Bible says that God did not send Jesus into the world to save the religious and the righteous, but for men and women like you and me – sinners. I want sinners everywhere to rejoice. Confess your sin and God will love you and change your life! If only you would tell Him, 'I know I've sinned but, Jesus, I need You. Thank You that You died for my sin. I want You to come into my life and change me.'

And Jesus will do it immediately.

CHAPTER TWENTY-EIGHT

DESPERATE FOR JESUS

I have tried to share with you some of the miracles of healing which are experienced in Russia, but inevitably people in the West say, 'God works miracles there, but it is not the same in our home churches.' Yet my experience has been that I have seen the same miracles in England and Germany, particularly so in Australia. No, not in the same numbers, but just as dramatic.

You ask me, 'Is there a difference then?' The answer is yes. I believe that with my own ministry there is a strong reason for these miracles – and remember that these do not just include healings.

In a TV interview in America, a well-known healing evangelist was asked what reason he could give for the miracles he sees in his meetings. His reply was that it was the atmosphere, the large numbers in the auditorium, the beautiful music and the awe-inspiring presence of the Holy Spirit. The same people asked me the identical question. I remembered the dusty stadiums in Russia and Ukraine, broken seats, poor amplification, thousands of people fighting to be touched by the Lord, crowds out of control, cries of desperation, shouts of despair. Helpless people, dirty bandages, open wounds, stinking diseases. The middle-aged looking so old because of their poverty and suffering. No medicines, no available doctors or hospitals. Over the whole stadium such a desperate sense that without this Jesus, if He is not alive, unless someone knows Him, there is no hope. My answer was this: the reason I see so many miracles is the desperate need of the people to find a real Jesus – and the desperation of Jesus to find the people who really want Him.

So many in the comfort of the West say to me, 'Pray for me, but if I am not healed I will go to the doctor, or the hospital. They will heal me!' This is not wrong, but in Russia they say, 'Pray for me. Without Christ I have no hope and I will die in pain!' They are desperate for Him. That's the difference!

In the Bible Jesus says, 'Behold I stand at the door and knock. If any man will open the door, I will come in!' (Revelation 3:20). Jesus is more willing to give than you are to receive. I sometimes say, 'Get into a race with God and try to out-give Him! You will never succeed in out-giving God, but the more you try, the more He will give you!'

The real life of faith, of being a Christian, of receiving either forgiveness or healing, is in knowing Him. I try to tell people how simple it is to receive Jesus. All you have to do is be like a drowning man: stop struggling, let go of your tiny piece of flotsam and come into His open arms. That wonderful hymn writer put it so powerfully: 'Just as I am without one plea, but that Thy blood was shed for me . . . I come.'

Healing, deliverance, forgiveness . . . stop struggling and

come into His arms! In Russia they want to be touched, they need to be loved, they want something personal. That's just how it is for us. So many of you who read this have secret problems which you cannot share. They are too deep, too hurtful, you cannot open up. But you need tell everything to Jesus. It's the only way to be healed, delivered, set free.

Talk to Him. He's listening. Ask Him to forgive your sin or to heal you. He loves you – He'll answer!

EUROVISION MISSION TO EUROPE

Eurovision Mission to Europe was founded by David Hathaway when God literally gave him a vision for Europe. This book has told the stories of the faith and the miracles that have followed his ministry from the very beginning.

As an evangelist, David's goal is to demonstrate who the REAL Jesus is. Everyone knows about religion, but many don't know WHO Jesus REALLY IS in the world today.

David's vision continues to grow and develop . . . but God's purposes can only be fulfilled through the continued support of individuals and churches. David says, 'I will not stop until we reach the whole of Russia and Europe with the Gospel of Jesus Christ. It takes revolutionary, triumphant faith that will overcome every challenge. But with God – and your support – we can do it!'

David Hathaway invites correspondence which should be addressed to:

Eurovision Mission to Europe
41 Healds Road
Dewsbury WF13 4HU
UK

Email: uk@propheticvision.org.uk

Eurovision Mission to Europe is a Registered Charity, No. 1013288

In the USA please contact:

Prophetic Vision USA INC
PO Box 10565
Wilmington
DE 19850
USA

Email: usa@propheticvision.org.uk

Federal ID #452–2050718

For further information on David's ministry, books and videos please visit: www.propheticvision.org.uk

PROPHETIC VISION MAGAZINE

David Hathaway's magazine, *Prophetic Vision*, is published worldwide. Its aim is to convey a strong vision concerning Europe, Russia and the Middle East especially Israel, clearly seeing God's strategy. The magazine demonstrates the power of God in action today – fulfilling prophecy – bringing revival – showing miracles. It will challenge you and stimulate you spiritually to become an active participant in the Fire of God!

Prophetic Vision is a British publication and is distributed free of charge four times a year in English, German, Danish/Norwegian, and some editions in Russian.

To receive your FREE copy please visit www.propheticvision.org.uk or contact:

Eurovision Mission to Europe
41 Healds Road
Dewsbury WF13 4HU
UK

Email: uk@propheticvision.org.uk

In the USA please contact:

Prophetic Vision USA INC
PO Box 10565
Wilmington
DE 19850

Email: usa@propheticvision.org.uk

DAVID HATHAWAY'S BOOKS

Why Siberia? – Hundreds of miracles happened when God called David to go to the end of the earth – spiritual adventure – life on the edge – very humorous – compelling reading! A challenging call to missions today!

Czech-Mate – Best-selling account of Bible smuggling – vivid portrayal of torture and triumph in a communist prison – midnight vision – answered prayer – dramatic miraculous rescue – faith in action!